AMAZING 7 MINUTE

◆ M E A L S ◆

OVER 100 RECIPIES READY IN
LESS THAN 7 MINUTES COOKING TIME

YVONNE STEPHENS

Skyhorse Publishing books may be purchased in bulk at special discounts for sales promotion, corporate gifts, fund-raising, or educational purposes. Special editions can also be created to specifications. For details, contact the Special Sales Department, Skyhorse Publishing, 307 West 36th Street, 11th Floor, New York, NY 10018 or info@skyhorsepublishing.com.

Skyhorse® and Skyhorse Publishing® are registered trademarks of Skyhorse Publishing, Inc.®, a Delaware corporation.

Visit our website at www.skyhorsepublishing.com.

10 9 8 7 6 5 4 3 2 1

Library of Congress Cataloging-in-Publication Data is available on file.

ISBN: 978-1-61608-812-5

Printed in China

About the author

Chef and world-traveler Yvonne Stephens was born in the Netherlands, and as a true Dutch woman, she traveled all over the world, from Latin-America, Asia, Hawaii, the Caribbean, and to most countries in Europe. The love of cooking comes from both her grandmother and mother, who cooked traditional Dutch cuisine and made fresh meals every day.

For hundreds of years, the Dutch ruled the spice trade from the Far East to Europe, and because Indonesia was part of the Dutch Royal Kingdom, the taste for Asian food, and creating dishes with a wide variety of herbs and spices, is characteristic of the Dutch.

The philosophy of *Amazing 7 Minute Meals* is to eat all six nutrients, educating the reader about herbs, spices, hard and soft vegetables, and about the benefits of fresh wholesome food. Using the ancient stir-fry technique, the recipes are cooked quickly, which results in slower digestion, thus resulting in fewer cravings and a greater balance of blood sugar levels. Due to the healthy ingredients, this book will help you fight cardiovascular diseases and lose weight.

Yvonne understands that lack of time is the main reason people eat fast food or grab a frozen meal. Sadly, most of those meals are prepared with preservatives, enriched flour, and the worst enemy for our body, trans fats.

Yvonne also knows that losing weight is a frustrating problem for people—and keeping it off is even worse. She conquered the eating disorder bulimia and has tried every diet possible, including the "prison diet" of bread and water. She has been yo-yoing—losing and gaining weight—for years. She has learned the real reason why diets do not work: You are starving your body of something it "needs." Most diets tell you to cut out nutrients your body needs, but this creates cravings.

As a former spinning, step, and kick box instructor, she learned that an active lifestyle combined with healthy eating is the only way is to lose weight and keep it off. Healthy eating doesn't mean that you have to eat like a rabbit or eliminate bread, rice, and pasta for the rest of your life. Yvonne explains all this in her book *Amazing 7 Minute Meals*.

As a graduate of the Art Institute of Philadelphia, Yvonne has a vast knowledge of ingredients and cooking techniques. Combining this knowledge with a love of food and the eagerness to learn everything about flavors and infusions, Yvonne has created more than 120 recipes that are ready in less than seven minutes cooking time. In this book, Yvonne will also teach you a few time-saving pre-prep tips and will provide advice to make grocery shopping fulfilling.

Amazing 7 Minute Meals brings you recipes from cuisines all over the world that are satisfying, but light. Now, your meals will be healthy, fast, and delicious, leaving more time for family and and other fun activities.

This is not a diet! The secret of weight loss and weight management is proper metabolism. The word metabolism comes from μεταβολισμος, the Greek word for "change." And that is what you can easily do… change your metabolism by making changes to your life style! Yvonne wants to help you make small, healthy changes that are successful, satisfying, and permanent with *Amazing 7 Minute Meals*.

"Knowing what's in your food
is the key to healthy
weight loss and
weight management.
Make it yourself:
No trans fats, no enriched flours,
no hidden chemicals;
just delicious flavors!

"This is what I will teach
you in *Amazing 7 Minute Meals.* "
—Yvonne Stephens

And the faster you cook it, the slower you will digest it!

Acknowledgements

Learning and sharing is part of life, but without the love and guidance of my husband, John, who also took the great photos in this book, my son Michael, my parents Wil and Piet, my father-in-law John, Sr., and my dog Trigger, I would not have been able to write this book and survive my eating disorder.

I also would like to thank my family in Portugal: Cindy, Paul, Coby, and my beloved brother-in-law Bill, who passed away, but looks down on me and keeps me going strong and proud of a day's work, even if the days don't go the way I want them to.

Special thanks to my friends Bob Bowersox of QVC, Bobbie Cappelli, my Thai friends Kanjana Overman and Aniwath Vadhanchai for supporting and encouraging me. And my friend and chef, Jeri Estok, for checking the recipes.

Trigger, while escorting me on one of our trips through Europe.

Special thanks also to:

Mathé and Léon Barendse of the greenhouses of

W. Barendse & Zn. in the Westland, Holland—The Greenery.com

Bruce Cobb of ARC Greenhouses, Shiloh, New Jersey,

The Chefs of the Art Institute of Philadelphia,

Breville Juicer

and everybody who I didn't mention by name but supported me and my family.

-Contents

A Few Ingredients

The Electric Wok

Buddha's Hand

Cherry Pepper

Shiitake Mushroom

Chinese or Garlic Chives

"Stir" Your Way to Health!

Introduction to Amazing 7 Minute Meals

Our Goal for You in Your Kitchen!

All recipes of the "Get Real with Healthy Eating" series are made with the freshest seasonal ingredients for the following reasons:

1) **Optimum flavor and health benefits:** Although dried spices and herbs are okay to use, fresh ones have more flavor and add more health benefits because they haven't lost any of these advantages in the drying process.

The Original Chinese Wok

2) **Health:** Veggies and herbs are loaded with disease-fighting powers: antioxidants, lipocene, pectin, and fiber, just to name a few. And when in-season, they are plentiful, full of flavor, and when prepared in a wok or other pan with stir-fry capability, the cook-time is so short that no valuable vitamins and minerals get lost. The fact is also that the quicker food is cooked, the slower it will be digested. So food that is prepared *al dente* makes your blood sugar level go up slower and not as high, creating fewer cravings and keeping you satisfied longer.

3) **Weight-loss:** The proportions for all recipes are to satisfy your body with the appropriate nutrition, healthy fats, low-sodium, herbs, and spices to help lower your blood pressure, lower your cholesterol, and help fight cardiovascular diseases. More about weight loss can be found on pages 6 and 7. Even if you changed 5 days a week to a diet using the *Amazing 7 Minute Meals* recipes, you'd reduce the intake of trans fats, enriched flours, and all other ingredients your body doesn't need when you want to improve your health and weight.

4) **Budget:** When veggies and herbs are in season, they are not only plentiful. They are also cheaper and, when harvested locally, they are more flavorful than the imported and/or grown all-year-around types. Using a wok to prepare food is not a new kitchen trend. The wok was invented more than a few thousand years ago in China. The sloped shape of the wok enables the heat to rise on the sides of the pan, providing the highest heat in the center, and less, but enough heat on the sides. Because the center of the heat is at the bottom of the pan, the food items have to be stirred around to use this heat but prevent the food from burning and sticking to the pan.

Culinary Travels

The advantages of using a wok to prepare your meals are that everything cooks fast; it is easy, making flavors are delicious and intense. But *Amazing 7 Minute Meals* doesn't just show you the culinary wealth of the Far East. Besides recipes from China, India, Indonesia, Japan, Korea, Malaysia, Singapore, and Vietnam, we also want to show you beautiful, colorful, and flavorful recipes from Hawaii, Europe, the Caribbean, South-America, and, in addition, the intriguing cuisine called *magreb*—cuisine from the area around Morocco, Tunisia, and Algeria.

Time & Budget Savers

We Show You What You Can Prepare in Minutes!

Take a journey through the cuisines of the world, embrace new flavors, and see that healthy cooking and delicious flavors are also easy and fast. A wok is used for stir-frying with just a little or no oil, boiling/stewing/braising (immersing in liquid), steaming (cooking with vapor), and frying (immersing in oil).

Every recipe shows how many meals it serves, plus the time it takes to do the PREP: pre-prepare the food before it goes into the pan. The COOK box on each recipe pages indicates the time it takes to heat the pan, add the food items, follow the steps, stir for the time recommended, and serve as indicated.

And although the recipes indicate "serve over rice; serve over noodles," etc., you can change that if you are in the mood for another side dish.

The Shopping List, on each recipe page, indicates exactly what you need and how to cut and slice it, but don't worry if you are missing an ingredient, the recipe can be adjusted, or you can just omit the missing ingredient. It will still be delicious.

Food items for this cooking technique are also available pre-cut, like meat or poultry, already cut up into strips or bite-size pieces, which reduces the PREP-time. There are bags of pre-cut, already washed veggies or containers of coarse chopped bell peppers or onions, so you don't have to do the crying.

Amazing 7 Minute Meals shows you how to buy ingredients and cut them up for your meals for today or later, which means you do the PREP a few days ahead of time and enjoy the short COOK time of only a few minutes. This is especially beneficial when you are in a hurry.

For example, on page 8, we show you a shopping list for four meals: *Bo Xao Ot Stir-fry*: a beef stir-fry with rice noodles (page 32); *Cod Stir-fry à la Normandy* with rosemary roasted potatoes (page 61); *Chicken & Veggie Stir-fry* with rice (page 124); and *Badhinjan Buran Stir-fry* with a tomato/cucumber salad (page 192). For ± $ 7.78 per person per meal, you have meals for 4 days with a PREP of ± 20 minutes total. 4 x COOK @ ± 5 minutes = 20 minutes. A total of 40 minutes, which is just 10 minutes per day to make delicious, healthy food! And you will even have some left-over ingredients to make a breakfast or small lunch.

Amazing 7 Minute Meals shows you what to do and what to use, but you can adjust a recipe if there is an ingredient in it that you are not too crazy about. Be creative, enjoy the short prep-and cook-time, and **Be Healthy!**

Serves 2 Dinners/3 Lunches

```
0:09        0:06
PREP        COOK
```

Pre-cut Vegetables & Stir-fry Packages

Prep: Cut, Store & Use When You Need It

Health & Weight Management

Stop Yo-yoing, Start Losing!

Losing and maintaining your weight is not an easy task, but when you start eating one of the *Amazing 7 Minute Meals* recipes every day, you will see that it is not an impossible task. We have created a wide variety of recipes so you can eat something you like, something that satisfies your nutritional needs and comforts your cravings. You can even make a different stir-fry for breakfast—the most important meal of the day.

Instead of standing in line at the drive-through, waiting for the food to be ready at the diner, or heating up a frozen dinner, you can make dinner in a few minutes, which leaves you with extra time for a walk or a bike ride.

Exercise is an important part of weight loss. Here are a few things that happen to you when you exercise:

- You will feel more energetic
- Your metabolism will increase
- Your blood pressure will lower
- Your cholesterol will lower
- Your muscles will get stronger
- Your cardiovascular strength will increase

A Few Things You Should Do

Have patience. Let your body get acquainted with changed eating habits. It will take up to 3 weeks before you will see your weight starting to drop, especially if you have been doing all types of restricted diets in the past.

Don't be afraid to try something new! Your taste buds and your muscles may have to get used to the changes you are making, but be adventurous and try new things!

Invite a friend for dinner! Ask a friend or colleague to come over for dinner and "wok" one of the more than 100 recipes from all over the world. After dinner, take a walk around the neighborhood. It's double the fun!

Measure your progress. Before you start making changes to increase your health and lose weight, take your measurements: chest, upper arm, waist, hip, thigh, and calf. Keep a little notebook, and take measurements at the same places every four weeks. You will be surprised!

Plan. MEP is the culinary term that means pre-prep your food. We call it PREP: plan your meals according to your schedule, shop for four days, pre-prep it, and enjoy the short COOK (cooking) time.

A Few Things You Should Avoid!

Don't step on the scale more than two times a month! When you start doing some lightweight training and walking, you will replace fat with muscles, and yes, muscles are heavier than fat. Concentrate on how you feel and how your clothes start to feel looser.

Avoid temptation! Don't buy foods you know you shouldn't eat. The willpower to resist a stack of cookies or a bag of potato chips is much easier when you don't have them in your pantry!

Avoid Cravings! When you eat something and feel hungry after less than one hour, your body gives you a signal that your food item was too high-glycemic. Next time you want to eat that same food item, combine it with a food item from the low-glycemic list.

Avoid being hungry! Don't wait untill you are hungry because your body will give off the wrong signals and you will eat too fast and too much. Take a little snack to avoid overeating!

Don't set major goals. Small steps bring you to the same result: success and a healthier body.

The Functions of the 6 Nutrients:

Your Body Cannot Function Properly without Them!

Nutrients are important compounds found in food. They all have their own roles in regulating specific body functions. They give the body energy and help build and rebuild tissue. Nutrients are vital compounds for every body cell. Without a balanced intake of nutrients, your body cannot function correctly: The brain will not function properly; nerves will not send accurate signals; digestion will not take place regularly; and muscles, bones, and even cells will not develop correctly.

So a balanced intake of food is necessary and vital! Limiting our intake with restricted diets often causes malnutrition, which can result in failing body functions in the short-term or over years: problems with bone density, bone and muscle strength, eye sight, even the risk of heart problems, or diabetes.

A short review of the 6 nutrients and their functions:

1. Carbohydrates—Carbohydrates supply energy to our bodies. They also provide bulk in the form of cellulose, which is needed for regular digestion and for digesting fats efficiently. High-glycemic foods or foods with simple sugars cause cravings. Those cravings can be seen as an addiction and are the main reason why people cannot stick to a no-carb or very low-carb diet. An increase in eating foods with a low glycemic level is proven to reduce the risk of developing diabetes and has shown a decrease in blood-sugar levels and a significant decrease in insulin resistance. This doesn't mean you should stop eating potatoes, noodles, or any other food items on the high-glycemic list. It means you should eat those food items combined with other foods on the low-glycemic list. The key is the 80/20 formula: 80 percent low-glycemic combined with 20 percent high-glycemic food items. See page 250 for more details.

2. Fats   Fats are nutrients responsible for rebuilding cell walls and the transportation of vitamins A, D, E, and K. Fat also insulates the body from heat, cold, and shock, and protects vital organs. Fat comes from various sources:

• *Poly-unsaturated fats*: corn oil, safflower, soy oil, sunflower, and fatty ocean fish (omega-3), like tuna or salmon.

• *Mono-unsaturated fats*: found in canola oil, olive oil, peanut oil, and in nuts.

• *Saturated fats*: in cheese, coconut oil, cream, fatty meat (fresh or processed), the skin and fat of poultry, lard, palm oil, full-fat ice cream, or whole milk.

• *Trans fats*: found in processed food, commercial baked products and fast food, shortening, and margarines. Trans fatty fats tend to raise bad cholesterol. Avoid these completely!

3. Protein—The function of proteins is to build hormones, muscles, tendons, hair, and nails and to help the immune system build antibodies. Proteins are made of amino acids, and they are vital for building a tremendous range of different structures and functions in our body, such as regulating the metabolic process by controlling the fluid balance in the cells. They also help build and repair tissues, enzymes, and some vitamins. Sources of protein are grain, dairy, soybean products, fish, meats, and many vegetables.

When people are suffering from malnutrition, the body stops certain functions, such as burning food for energy, producing certain hormones, or repairing cells.

4. **Vitamins**—The function of vitamins is to work as our body's regulators, needed in minute amounts, for growth, maintenance, and reproduction.

• *Vitamin A* helps prevent night-blindness, and promotes good vision in general. It helps keep your skin smooth and free from blemishes. It promotes growth and helps mucus membranes stay healthy.

• *Vitamin B* helps the body with a whole range of functions: *Niacin* helps keep the nervous system healthy. *Riboflavin* helps cells use oxygen. *Thiamine* helps promote the appetite and digestion. It is a fighter against cortisol, the hormone that makes us overeat. It regulates the nervous system and prevents irritability. It helps form co-enzymes needed for breaking down carbohydrates. The main function is to help the body release energy from food.

• *Vitamin C* helps our immune system fight infections and helps protect our body from free radicals and cancer. This powerful vitamin helps wounds heal, bruises clear up, and broken bones mend. Vitamin C is the "cement material" that holds body cells together. Vitamin C also improves the absorption of iron.

• *Vitamin D* builds strong bones and teeth in children and maintains strong bones in adults. Good sources of vitamin D are sunlight, butter, fatty fish, meat, and eggs.

• *Vitamin E* is a fat-soluble vitamin that provides protection from the effects of free radicals, which are potentially damaging to the body's cells. Free radicals are proven to cause cardiovascular diseases and cancer.

• *Vitamin K* helps prevent blood clots. Sources are: asparagus, cauliflower, green vegetables, and lean meat. Vitamin A, D, E, and K are fat-soluble vitamins, and can be stored in the body. Vitamin C and the B-complex vitamins are water-soluble vitamins and must be replaced daily.

5. **Minerals**—The function of minerals is building our bones, teeth, tissues, and body fluids. Minerals are needed to regulate body processes:

• *Calcium* helps blood clot and keeps heart muscles and nerves working properly. Calcium also improves bone-density and promotes stronger teeth. Sources are: broccoli, cabbage, cheese, greens, meat, milk, oysters, potatoes, salmon, sardines, soy-based products, tofu, and yogurt.

• *Iron* can be seen as a blood and energy booster found in beans, legumes, peas, sardines, sesame seeds, shellfish (like clams, mussels, shrimp, and oysters), spinach, turkey meat, and whole-wheat bread.

• *Magnesium* helps the nervous system work properly, regulates our body's temperature, helps muscles contract, and also helps cells produce energy. Resources are: cheese, milk, vegetables, and whole-wheat bread.

• *Phosphorus* helps balance the alkalis and acids in the blood. Sodium, chloride, and potassium are needed together to control osmosis (the process of water flow in and out of the cells through the cell walls). Minerals also affect brain function, nerve impulses, and functions of involuntary muscles like our heart.

6. **Water**—Sixty percent of our body mass is water. Our body maintains its water balance by routinely sending signals to drink and to urinate. When the body is sweating, the body also indicates that it needs water to prevent dehydration. It helps the growth, lubrication, and maintenance of cells and tissue. Water also regulates our digestive system and flushes out all chemical waste produced by our kidneys. Drinking a few glasses of water a day helps you lose weight.

A Few Suggestions for a Healthy Diet

A balanced nutritional plan is the key to providing your body with the nutrients it needs to function properly. These are a few examples of days with balanced, healthy, delicious, nutritious, and satisfying food that will also help you lose weight and keep it off. To prevent cravings, choose 80 percent low-glycemic and 20 percent high-glycemic. And most important: DO NOT SKIP A MEAL!

1

Breakfast
2 slices of multi-grain toast with jelly, a slice of cheese or lunch meat
½ grapefruit
1 cup of coffee or tea

Lunch
A mixed green salad with pine nuts and garlic-yogurt dressing
1 cup easily made soup, see Ch. 10

Dinner
Asian Fish Stir-fry

Plus
1 small handful of nuts as a mid-afternoon snack
green tea, blueberry iced tea

And
A brisk 10 minute walk while your rice is cooking…

2

Breakfast
wok-infusion breakfast
1 glass pomegranate/orange juice
1 cup of coffee or tea

Lunch
A Korean fish salad with ginger dressing

Dinner
Italian Veal Stir-fry

Plus
⅓ cup of pineapple salsa with a handful of tri-color tortilla chips as a mid-afternoon snack
1 cup of yogurt with fresh fruit
green tea, blueberry iced tea

And
A brisk 10 minute walk while your pasta is cooking…

3

Breakfast
1 cup of yogurt with cinnamon and 3 T muesli
1 kiwi
1 boiled egg
1 cup of coffee or tea

Lunch
Bouillabaisse Stir-fry

Dinner
Indian Veggie Stir-fry

Plus
4 multi-grain crackers with a piece of Leyden *pitjes* (cumin seeds) cheese
1 glass pomegranate/orange juice

And
A brisk 10 minute walk while your rice noodles are soaking…

4

Breakfast
soy-yogurt-fruit smoothie
1 cup of hot green tea

Lunch
1 cup black bean soup, see Ch. 10
⅓ cup salsa
handful of tortilla chips

Dinner
Hawaiian Fish Stir-fry

Plus
1 small handful of soy nuts as a mid-afternoon snack
1 apple or peach
green tea, blueberry iced tea

And
A brisk 10 minute walk while your rice is cooking…

5

Breakfast
stir-fry breakfast
1 glass pomegranate/orange juice
1 cup of coffee or tea

Lunch
Shrimp Stir-fry

Dinner
Spanish Beef Stir-fry
small side salad of tomato, cucumber, and olives

Plus
4 multi-grain crackers with a piece of Brie (French cheese)
1 cup of yogurt with fresh fruit
green tea, blueberry iced tea

And
A brisk 10 minute walk while your pasta or potatoes are cooking…

Time & Health Savers
Take Control of Your Life!

Here is a shopping list for four meals with a variety of flavors and delicious, fresh ingredients:

Bo Xao Ot Stir-fry: a beef stir-fry with rice noodles, page 32

Cod Stir-fry à la Normandy with rosemary roasted potatoes, page 61

Chicken & Veggie Stir-fry with rice, page 124

Badhinjan Buran Stir-fry with a tomato/cucumber salad, page 192.

The total of these fresh ingredients is $62.21, so for ± $7.78 per person per meal, you have 8 meals for 4 days with a PREP of ± 20 minutes total, 4 x COOK @ ± 5 minutes = 20 minutes. A maximum of 40 minutes, which is just 10 minutes per day to make delicious, healthy food! And you will even have some left-over ingredients to make a breakfast or small lunch. Soon this PREP time will be even shorter because you will be able to buy more varieties of fresh pre-cut, ready-to-use veggies. Just ask for them at your produce or grocery store.

Amazing 7 Minute Meals is a lifestyle change you have been waiting for. No new diet restrictions, which are just another unhealthy way to lose weight and then gain it back again. All you need are the goods of "Mother Nature," prepared in a few minutes, keeping all the good nutrients in it for you! **Just Honest Food!**

Shopping list-for all 4 recipes:

Produce:

1 lb. eggplant	@ $ 1.99/lb.	=	$	1.99	
1 bag baby carrots	@ $ 1.09/ea.	=	$	1.09	
1 lb. broccoli florets	@ $ 3.49/lb.	=	$	3.49	
4 oz. snap Peas	@ $ 3.99/lb.	=	$	1.00	
1 green bell pepper	@ $ 0.99/lb.	=	$	1.09	
1 yellow bell pepper	@ $ 2.99/lb.	=	$	2.61	
1 red bell pepper	@ $ 1.99/lb.	=	$	1.99	
1 orange bell pepper	@ $ 2.99/lb.	=	$	2.99	*
1 hot pepper	@ $ 0.99/lb.	=	$	0.31	
3 tomatoes	@ $ 3.99/lb.	=	$	4.79	
1 shallot	@ $ 0.79/ea.	=	$	0.79	
1 container onions, diced	@ $ 2.99/ea.	=	$	2.99	*
1 lb. broccoli florets	@ $ 3.49/lb.	=	$	3.49	*
1 cucumber	@ $ 2.50/ea.	=	$	2.50	*
1 stick lemongrass	@ $ 1.99/lb.	=	$	0.39	*
1 bunch parsley	@ $ 0.99/ea.	=	$	0.99	*
1 piece ginger	@ $ 1.29/lb.	=	$	0.77	*
1 bunch rosemary	@ $ 1.99/ea.	=	$	1.99	*
1 lb. potatoes	@ $ 2.99/5 lb.	=	$	1.20	*
1 lemon	@ $ 0.25/ea.	=	$	0.25	
garlic	@ $ 0.79/ea.	=	$	0.79	*

Dairy:

8 oz. yogurt, plain	@ $ 0.69/ea.	=	$	0.69	
4 oz. goat cheese	@ $ 2.59/ea.	=	$	0.65	*

Meat/fish/poultry:

10 oz. lean beef	@ $ 9.99/lb.	=	$	6.25
1 lb. cod	@ $ 8.99/lb.	=	$	8.99
10 oz. chicken breast	@ $ 9.99/lb.	=	$	6.25

Basic Pantry:

salt	@ $ 0.50/ea.	=	$	0.03	
pepper	@ $ 0.60/ea.	=	$	0.04	
star anise, ground	@ $ 3.49/ea.	=	$	0.15	
coriander	@ $ 2.49/ea.	=	$	0.06	
rice noodles	@ $ 1.79/ea.	=	$	0.80	
low sodium soy sauce	@ $ 2.69/ea.	=	$	0.45	*
fish sauce	@ $ 1.79/ea.	=	$	0.38	*
Total groceries		=	$	62.21	

1 x MEP `0:20`   WOK PER DAY `0:05`

That is 8 dinners @ $ 7.78 per dinner, or 12 lunches @ $ 5.18 per lunch.

A Few Simple Guidelines

Control Your Time & Budget in Detail

We will introduce you to hot peppers, sweet or bell peppers, herbs, spices, fruits and vegetables from all over the world, plus cooking tips to help you make a meal in no time. We will show you that ingredients can be "cross-used" not limited to the country or cuisine of origin.

When you prepare your own food, you know what you put in it, and can be sure that you are serving something healthy food without trans fats, preservatives, chemical coloring agents, or flavor enhancers.

The food you prepare contains fresh ingredients and is loaded with health benefits. Eating healthy will also help you maintain a proper weight, and if you have decided to start cooking more to lose weight, this program is your key to success.

The original Chinese wok carries the seasonings, spices, and flavors from all the previous meals as a tasty history. The modern non-stick coated wok is used for more than indigenous meals, so it will wash away any hints of the previous meal; they should not interfere with the flavors of today's meal. We are "wokking" today, but any large skillet will be a good alternative. Just follow the steps below.

Step 1. Gather Your Ingredients

Step 2. Cut Your Ingredients to Desired Size

Step 3. Heat Wok/Pan to Desired Temperature. Add Oil or Spray with Cooking Spray

Step 4. Add Ingredients That Need the Longest Cooking Time

Step 5. Add Rest of Ingredients, Spices, Herbs and Seasoning

Enjoy!

Hot Peppers

Studies have shown that adding spices—especially chiles—temporarily boosts our metabolism by about 25 percent. A chili or pepper comes in green, yellow, orange, red, and black. The color does not always indicate increasing hotness, but "the larger the pod, the milder it is" is a steady rule. To decrease the hotness, you can remove the seeds and membranes, which contain 80 percent of the capsaicin responsible for the intensity of the chile. Adding chiles to your dishes also helps as a decongestion aid. Wearing gloves is advisable; this reduces the risk of rubbing and touching skin and eyes, which can be very painful.

Anaheim Chili—The mildest and most commonly available chili in the United States. ± 6-8" x 2" fruit, with a thick and crispy bright green color that turns to red and hotter when ripened. Used grilled or roasted for salsas, stews, and soups, or stuffed (*chiles rellenos*). Heat-index 2.

Banana Pepper—A banana-shaped sweet pepper with an average size of 6" x 2¼", used for stir-frying, salsas, and grilling. Heat-index 0.

Caribbean Chile—This red, ripe version of the regular habanero has a similar fiery shape and heat, with a glossy and iridescent skin. Heat-index 10.

Cherry Pepper—A small, round pepper with an average diameter of 1½"–2" in bright red. A slightly sweet flavor ranging from mild to medium-hot. Used fresh or pickled. Heat-index 1.

Chipotle Chili—A dried, smoked jalapeño with a wrinkled, dark brown skin. Chipotles can be found dried, pickled, and canned. Used in adobo sauce, stews, and pickled. Heat-index 4.

Cubanelle—A long, tapered, thick-walled, waxy, semi-sweet pepper, ranging in color from yellow to red. It is 3-lobed, 6" x 2", and tapers to a blunt end. Used as a frying pepper. Heat-index 0.

Fresno Chili—Waxy, two-inch pods ripen from green (spicy) to red (sweeter). The Fresno chili pepper is often mistaken for a red jalapeño, but the Fresno is broader at the top and is hotter than the jalapeño. Use in soups, piquant sauces, and pickles. Heat-index 4.

Habanero Chili—This small, lantern-shaped chili is a super-hot native to the Caribbean, the Yucatan, and the northern coast of South America. The habanero grows to an average of 2" x 1¼" wrinkled ranging from light green to bright orange when ripe. Heat-index 10.

Hot Paper Lantern—An ultra-hot chili, also called long hot pepper, 3"–4" long, elongated and wrinkled lantern-shaped, growing from bright lime green to orange or scarlet red. Heat-index 10.

Hungarian Wax Chili—A large yellow hot pepper with 5½" x 1½" smooth, waxy fruit tapering to a point. The flavor ranges from mild to medium-hot. Hungarian wax chiles are also called banana chiles. Its sunset-ripening colors from yellow to orange to red make them the prettiest pickling peppers. Heat-index 5.

Heat-index	
0	Negligible Scoville Units
1	100–1,000 SU
2	1,000–1,500 SU
3	1,500–2,500 SU
4	2,500–5,000 SU
5	5,000–15,000 SU
6	15,000–30,000 SU
7	30,000–50,000 SU
8	50,000–100,000 SU
9	100,000–350,000 SU
10	350,000–855,000 SU

A Few Examples

Anaheim Chile

Banana Pepper

Caribbean Chile

Cherry Pepper

Jalapeño Chili—Dark green chiles range from hot to very hot; the seeds and veins especially are extremely hot. The color changes to red when mature. Available fresh and canned, used in sauces, stuffed with cheese and deep-fried. Jalapeños are called chipotles when dried and smoked. Heat-index 4.

Pepperoncini—A thin, 2"–3" long chile with a bright green, wrinkled color. They have a slightly sweet flavor which can range from medium to medium-hot. This pepper is also called a Tuscan pepper, and is most commonly available in jars, packed in a water, vinegar, and salt brine. Pepperoncini's are perfect for cold antipasti, stuffed, mixed in salads, and as a pizza topping. Heat-index 4.

Pimiento; Pimento—A large, red, heart-shaped sweet pepper that measures 4"–6" long and 1½"–2" wide. Pimiento is Spanish for "pepper." The sweet, succulent and very aromatic bell pepper is used canned and bottled (halves, strips, or pieces), but is especially used dried and ground into tasty red paprika powder. Heat-index 0.

Poblano Chili—A mild, pungent, slightly sweet flavor. Great for stuffing, and roasted while still black-green. The darker the color, the richer the flavor. This chili is about 2½"–3 "wide and 4"–5" long, tapering from top to bottom in a triangular shape. Heat-index 4.

Scotch Bonnet Chili—An irregularly, lamp-shaped chili, which ranges in color from yellow to orange to red and is 1"–1½". The Scotch bonnet is closely related to the habanero, also one of the hottest of the chiles. Heat-index 10.

Serrano Chili—A small, slightly-pointed chili with a very hot, savory flavor. As it matures, its smooth, bright green skin turns scarlet red then yellow. Available canned, pickled, or packed in oil, sometimes with carrots, onions, or other vegetables. The dried serrano chili is available fresh and as a powder called *chile seco* and is generally used in sauces. Heat-index 7.

Thai Chili—The small, slender, thin-fleshed Thai chili ranges in color from green to red when fully ripe. A fiery heat that doesn't dissipate with cooking, with an average size about 1"–1½" long and ¼" in diameter. Heat-index 9.

Remember! Wear gloves when you clean peppers. To decrease the hotness of a pepper, you can remove the seeds and membranes, which contain 80 percent of the capsaicin responsible for the hotness. Rubbing your skin or eyes can become very painful. Rinse the area you touched with water until the burning is gone!

Cubanelle

Fresno Chile

Hot Paper Lantern

Hungarian Wax Chile

Poblano Chile

Serrano Chile

Thai Chile

11

Sweet or Bell Pepper

A heavy, thick pepper ranging in color from pale to dark green, from yellow to orange to red, purple to brown to black. Most commonly used are the bell peppers, so-called because of their bell-like shape. The flesh is mild, sweet, crisp and juicy. The size and shape vary from 3" to 5" long and from 2" to 4" wide. Great for stuffing, roasting, grilling, and in soups or stews.

They are a great source of vitamin C, small amounts of vitamin A and calcium, phosphorus, iron, riboflavin, thiamine, and niacin. Of all sweet peppers, the orange has the mildest taste. It is juicy and refreshing—like a healthy thirst-quencher. Even children will like this mild flavor served raw as a snack. The orange pepper is unparalleled for health. Heat-index 0.

The possibilities for using bell peppers are unlimited. We only touch on a few here, but you will find that we use them a lot in our recipes because they are so flavorful and healthy. Bell peppers can be used in every type of cuisine: Italian, julienned in spaghetti or any other type of pasta; Spanish, julienned in paella, roasted and marinated, served as a salad with olives; Hungarian, chopped or julienned in Hungarian Goulash, soups and stews; French, diced or julienned in soups and stews; Asian, stir-fried in diced pieces or julienned; Mexican, sautéed with fajitas; Caribbean, grilled, sautéed, etc.

per 3½ oz./100 g fruit	Orange	Banana	Sweet pepper (paprika)			
			green	red	yellow	orange
kiloJoule	193	364	67	92	92	92
kilocal	46	87	16	22	22	22
protein (mg)	0	0	1	1	1	1
fat (g)	0	0	0	0	0	0
carbohydrate (g)	14	22	3	4,5	4,5	4,5
calcium (mg)	8	4	15	15	15	15
iron (mg)	0,24	0,24	0,5	0,5	0,5	0,5
sodium (mg)			5	6	6	6
vitamin A (mg)	0,01	0,01	100	120	120	160
vitamin B1 (mg)	0	0	30	30	30	30
vitamin B2 (mg)	0	0	70	70	70	70
vitamin C (mg)	51	9	70	165	175	180

Bell peppers should be firm and glossy when you buy them, the skin unwrinkled without sunken or soft spots. Cut the peppers lengthwise, remove the seeds and cores, wash them, and then prepare as desired.

Any type (color) of bell pepper can be roasted, grilled, marinated, baked, blanched, or stuffed whole.

Bell peppers can be used as garnish, in salads, on sandwiches, and especially with the orange bell pepper, as a snack. A fresh bell pepper keeps for about one week in the refrigerator. Take a look at the recipes by The Greenery at www.the-greenery.com.

Spinach Stuffed Bell Pepper,
The Greenery

Bell Pepper Pizza,
The Greenery

Stuffed Bell Peppers,
The Greenery

Stuffed Baby Bell Pepper,
The Greenery

Promote Food with Extra Health Benefits

The sweet pepper is part of the hot pepper family. It's a nightshade plant, grown in the greenhouses of Mathé and Léon Barendse in the Westland, Holland. The company W. Barendse & Zn. grows orange bell peppers to export to the United States, Canada, and all over Europe. The orange peppers are planted and picked from February until December without the use of artificial light. The taste of the sweet pepper is not hot, as the name indicates, but sweet, juicy, crisp, and refreshing.

Sweet Pepper

A Great Snack, a Colorful Addition to Your Salads

The process of growing orange peppers is very controlled, and with a method called "biological crop protection," the use of chemicals is sporadic. The peppers never come in contact with chemicals, as the period between chemical usage and harvest is restricted. The fruit does not need to be washed before being sold. Washing often causes some damage to the fruit and will remove the natural protective layer of the fruit. This layer gives peppers a better quality and a longer shelf life. The Dutch pepper, for example, is always clean, is of a high quality, is safe, and has a long shelf life. So look for these "Orange Miracles" at your grocery store. For more information check: www.sweet-orange-bell-pepper.nl.

W. Barendse & Zn.
Westland, Holland

Look What "Mother Nature" Has to Offer

All that grows in the ARC Greenhouses in Shiloh, New Jersey, grows with the grace of "Mother Nature" and the technology developed by Bruce Cobb, owner of ARC Greenhouses. Bruce and his family have been in the business of growing since 1984. ARC Greenhouses is dedicated to a program of improved sustainability and has made major innovations in product development and system design. All the plants—full-size or micro, herbs or lettuces—are beautiful examples of what "Mother Nature" has to offer for our menu. The cleanliness of this growing method, and the isolation of crops, provides worthwhile protection from spreading diseases. A wide variety of colorful and flavorful produce is available year-round. ARC Greenhouses provides high-quality produce, shipped fresh all over the country six days a week.

Hydroponics is a Technology that Gives New Meaning to Eating Lettuce and Herbs

Hydroponics is growing plants in nutrient-enhanced water. ARC Greenhouses uses a system called recirculating hydroponics. In this system, the water is channeled through troughs or tubes in which plants are placed so that their roots can absorb what they need from a properly formulated nutrient solution. When the excess water and nutrients leave these channels, they return to a tank where the fertilizer solution is readjusted to maintain a constant balance. This system has a distinct environmental advantage: none of the chemicals are allowed to go into the ground, which means that nitrogen can't build up in ground water—a major factor in the contamination of America's waterways.

ARC Greenhouses, Shiloh, NJ; Bruce Cobb and assistant Tina

Plants That Grow in Water Taste Better

Bruce Cobb of ARC Greenhouses explains why he believes that plants grown in water taste better. "It is because healthy plants taste better. Healthy plants require healthy roots. Roots obtain the nutrients that plants need. With hydroponics, the roots always have a good supply of the necessary nutrients. This is especially true with micro-nutrients, those essential trace elements such as iron, zinc, and copper that must be present in minute doses for a plant to thrive. While it is relatively simple to provide the basic NPK nutrients (nitrogen, phosphorus, potassium), it is another matter to deliver the delicate balance of micro-nutrients—and we believe it is these that define the flavor.

"Our system maintains the optimum quantities of these essentials in its continuous flow. At the same time, the roots of our plants receive an ample supply of water for the important process of transpiration, which enables the leaves to hold a constant, safe temperature. In addition, this steady flow carries an endless supply of oxygen to the roots. Oxygen is of course vital to healthy growth, and since our plants are placed in such a way that a part of each root is in water and the rest is in air, there is never a lack of this requirement," said Cobb.

It should be noted that many of the enemies of plants live in soil where they can attack plants in the root zone where they feed. Research has shown that roots are better able to fight off unhealthy organisms and that the quality of the plant is superior when water supply is optimum, thus contributing to an abundance of healthy micro-life. Simply stated, plants grown this way are healthier and taste better. Check their website for more information: www.arcgreenhouses.com

Basil—A fresh herb that comes in a wide variety, is but oh so flavorful. Opal, Thai, regular basil, etc. all have a few things in common: intense flavor, great health benefits, and add a different dimension to food. See pages 10–11.

Chiles—Hot and spicy, used in Asian, Mexican, and Latin American dishes. See pages 4–7.

Galangal—A family member of the ginger root, but harder and pinker flesh. More information about spices, page 12–15.

A few unfamiliar examples:

Buddha's hand—A member of the citrus family, but only the zest is edible. There is no flesh.

Cactus Pear—The fruit of the several cactuses is also called prickly pear, and the dark-red flesh tastes like a sweet melon.

Durian—This large fruit of the Malaysian tree has a hard, pointy shell with soft, sweet, creamy flesh.

Because of the fruit's smell, it is only available in the United States canned and dried, not fresh. *Amazing 7 Minute Meals* shows you which ingredients you can use, and how to **Be Creative!**

A Few Examples

Hydroponics: A Few Days Old

Hydroponics: A Beautiful Arugala

Perfect Butter Head Lettuce

Vibrant Red Amaranth

Buddha's Hand

Cactus Pear

Durian

15

The Benefits and Flavors of Herbs

Basil

When you buy leaves, seeds, flowers, or roots, or when you harvest them at the farmer's market or from your own vegetable garden, you can dry them to add that delicious aroma to all your food items year-round. Traditionally, herbs were hung upside-down in the attic or in the kitchen near the hearth where the heat of the fire would dry them slowly, allowing the herbal oils to flow down into the leaves. When the herbs are dry, you can take them off the stems, chop them and pack them in bags to freeze or put in herb jars to use later.

When using dried herbs, only use half the amount indicated in the recipe for fresh herbs. Add dried herbs at the beginning of the cooking process, and add fresh herbs about 5–10 minutes before serving to preserve freshness. Adding fresh herbs to your dishes not only enhances the flavors, but also adds a wide variety of health benefits, like vitamins, minerals, etc.

Caraway

Basil—Basil has a rich, robust and spicy, mildly peppery flavor with the aroma of mint.

Bay Leaves—Strengthens the intensity of soups, stews, and sauces. Mostly used whole; remove before serving.

Caraway—The leaves and seeds have a strong aromatic flavor. The root is a winter vegetable.

Cilantro

Chervil—Chervil leaves are soft and light, fern-like with a flavorful mix of parsley and anise.

Chives—Tastes like an onion and looks like a small leek with a hint of garlic.

Chinese Chives—Longer and thicker than regular chives, with thick white, edible flowering buds.

Chinese or Garlic Chives

Cilantro—The leaves have a bold flavor of strong sage and a bit of lemon. Also called coriander.

Chocolate Mint—This bright green, purple-tinged mint tastes like an innuendo of chocolate.

Dill—An herb with a dominant flavor: fresh or dried, always added near the end of cooking, especially with fish.

Garlic

Fennel—This herb tastes like a softer and nuttier version of anise.

Garlic Bulb or Cloves—Powerful, robust, and oniony, is an excellent description for the garlic bulb. Broken in cloves, chopped, minced, or pureed, this spice is important in most of the world's cuisine's, and it gives a distinct characteristic to all foods except desserts. Also available dried in flakes, or in powder, but fresh is preferable. This is one of the examples of disease-preventive foods in our kitchen. The Chinese have long used garlic to treat high blood pressure and other cardiac or circulatory ailments and certain cancers.

Ginger

Ginger—The flavor seems to be half spice and half citrus. The root of the plant is used fresh or dried in the recipes of Southeast Asia, the Caribbean, and North Africa. Add it to fruit, meats, poultry, fish; combine it with onions and garlic; or use in quick breads, cakes, and cookies.

Horseradish

Horseradish—The root has a sharp, mustardy flavor, is grated and served with beef and fish dishes.

Kaffir Lime Leaf—This leaf looks like two joined, wide bay leaves, but the flavor is distinctive and intense. The leaf is used in Hawaiian and Asian cuisine.

Lavender—Pale green leaves with bright purple flowers add a pungent flavor to your dishes.

Lemon basil—Same shape and leaves as regular basil, but with a distinct lemon flavor.

Lemon Grass—The fibrous leaves have a stiff midrib and sharp edges; use finely chopped.

Lemongrass

Lemon Verbena—The long, narrow leaves of this herb have an overpowering lemon flavor.

Marjoram—Tastes and looks like oregano, but is subtler and sweeter, with a hint of balsam.

Marjoram

Mint—Curly mint and spearmint are very popular varieties of less common species like orange and pineapple mint. Use chopped leaves, or use sprigs as beautiful decoration.

Micro-greens—Micro-greens are small representations of salad greens, herbs, edible flowers, and leafy vegetables. Used as garnishes, or additions of flavor.

Mirco-corn shoots

Opal Basil—The purple leaves have a pungent flavor: a mixture of licorice and cloves.

Oregano—The peppery taste is similar to marjoram, but more powerful and aromatic.

Parsley—A mega-fighter! A major source of Vitamin A, B, and C, calcium, and iron. Parsley is a gently flavored addition.

Opal Basil

Rosemary—The pungent, pine-y herb is powerful, sweet with a slight ginger flavor.

Sage—Aromatic, soft gray-green leaves with an intense taste, a bit lemony when fresh and a bit stronger when dried.

Savory—A green leaf herb with a delicate peppery flavor, also called "bean herb."

Tarragon—A subtle licorice flavored herb. Do not cook it longer than 15 minutes to prevent from turning bitter.

Pineapple mint

Thyme—Thyme has a delicate green flavor with a faint clove aftertaste. The flavor increases when cooked.

Wheatgrass—An herb or a lettuce, or neither? Wheatgrass is a great source of enzymes and vitamins, cleaning agents that help the body lower the blood pressure, and it fights infections. It even works as an appetite suppressant. An awesome small addition to a salad with very big health benefits. Grasses come in a wide variety of flavors: pepper grass, barley grass, and even sea grasses.

Rosemary

Spice Up Your Dishes

Spices are great flavoring agents, and even greater alternatives to sodium. Be creative with the bold, intense flavors. Check out the chart of indigenous herbs and spices. Dried herbs and spices are usually more intensely flavored, so when using dried instead of fresh, use half of the amount indicated in the recipe. These are just a few examples used in stir-fries.

Allspice—Ground berries that taste like a blend of cinnamon, cloves, and nutmeg.

Anise Star and Seed—The leaves and seed have a distinctive, sweet licorice flavor.

Arrowroot Starch—White silky powder used to thicken sauces, and gravies.

Basil—Most popular herb in dried, chopped leaves, which we like to use in soups, stews, or salads.

Caraway Seeds—A flavor-enhancer, lightly toast the seed before using; can also be freshly ground for use in carrots, potato, and cabbage dishes.

Cardamom—An ancient spice native to India used mostly as a dessert spice in the West due to the warm, sweet, spicy flavor.

Cayenne Pepper—A bright red, hot, pungent chili usually used dried. Heat-index 5–7.

Chili Powders—Chili powders are blends of one or more chiles. They come in different strengths, and the color can be yellow to red, to red-brown and black, depending on the peppers used.

Chinese 5-Spice Powder—A salt-free, Chinese spice blend: equal parts star anise, Szechwan peppercorn, cinnamon, cloves, and fennel seeds. A very bold blend, so use sparingly.

Chives—Frozen and freeze-dried chives give garden freshness to all types of dishes.

Cilantro Leaves, Dried—This leaf of the coriander plant is used in many dishes.

Cinnamon—The flavor is piquant and slightly sweet; used in baking and desserts, but also an essential ingredient for all types of dishes in Indonesian, Arabic, Mexican, and Greek cuisine.

Cloves—A reddish brown, dried, unopened flower bud of the tropical evergreen clove tree. These small buds are used ground or whole and have a sharp, distinctive, wintergreen-like flavor.

Coriander—The tiny light brown-yellow seeds are mildly fragrant and have an aromatic flavor.

Cumin—A fiery, slightly bitter tasting, somewhat nutty-flavored seed of an herb indigenous to the Mediterranean region.

Curry Powders—A yellowish spice blend with up to 20 different spices, ground seeds, and herbs, like nutmeg, mace, cardamom, fennel seed, and turmeric, which gives it the yellow color. Curry is indigenous to India; used in many Indian dishes, such as an East-Indian sauce called curry; a spicy, gravy-like sauce is made with peppers, onion, etc.

Dill—Dill has a dominant personality and a well-rounded tang, especially used in fish, lamb, and vegetable dishes. Also available ground.

A Few Examples

Star Anise

Cardamon

Cayenne Pepper

Chives, dried

Cloves

Coriander Seeds

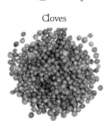

Cumin Seeds

Epazote—Epazote has a subtle, slightly sweet flavor, used in Mexican and Latin-American dishes.

Fenugreek—A bit bitter, but sweet and definitely a strong spice; used in curries and Indian dishes.

Fenugreek

Flax Seed—Flax seed was re-discovered in the kitchen as a mega-source of the plant version of omega-3s called alpha-linolenic acid. The flax plant has been used in Asia and Europe since at least 6,000 B.C. Medical research has proven that adding omega-3s to your diet has tremendous health benefits. Just ¼ cup of flaxseed-meal gives the same health benefits of about 30 cups of fresh broccoli. Flaxseed is considered a digestive aid. Use it as flaxseed meal in stir-fries, soups, and stews or as flaxseed oil in dressings and sauces. Flax seed has a nutty, mild flavor.

Flax Seed

Galangal Root—Best known as Thai ginger, galangal is a tuber similar in appearance to ginger, but not in flavor or texture. Also available in powder called Laos.

Herbes de Provence—Beautiful mix of herbs: dried rosemary, marjoram, basil, savory, and thyme; used in soups, stews, meat dishes, pastas, and salads.

Galangal Root

Hyssop Herb—Hyssop has been used in the Middle East for centuries. Its main value was in preserving meat and as a cleansing herb. It is one of the herbs traditionally used to flavor Chartreuse liqueur. Hyssop may relieve congestion and dispel gas.

Jalapeño—Jalapeño peppers are freshly ground to make this popular powder. You can add ground jalapeño to virtually any dish to give it a nice peppery zing. Heat-index 5.

Hyssop Herb

Italian Herbs—A blend of dried basil, thyme, oregano, marjoram, rosemary, garlic, crushed red pepper, and fennel seed. This herb/spice blend is great to experiment with in other recipes.

Kaffir Lime Leaf—This leaf looks like two joined, wide bay leaves, but the flavor is distinctive and intense. The leaf is used in Hawaiian and Asian cuisine. Dried rind is also available.

Mace, dried—Mace is indigenous to the Pacific. It is the outer shell (web) of the nutmeg, which is shredded or ground to create mace. It is used in fish dishes, meat stuffing, and pickling.

Mace

Nutmeg—Nutmeg is native to Indonesia; it has a distinctive, pungent fragrance and a warm, slightly sweet taste. It has unlimited uses including baked goods, meats, sausages, sauces, or vegetables.

Onion, Dried—These dehydrated chopped onions will give the taste of fresh onions to any of your dishes: beef, chicken, vegetable, soup, or stew. Rehydrating is simple: just soak in a little liquid—stock or water. Available dried or as a powder.

Onion, dried

Oregano—There are two types of oregano: Greek oregano is used in European cooking, and Mexican oregano for Mexican cuisine. Mexican oregano is stronger and not quite as sweet. Oregano is available dried and ground.

Paprika—There are three types of the dark vibrant red powder called paprika: Hungarian paprika has the richest flavor and is sweet with a rich aroma, and Californian has the best color-use for meats and goulash. Spanish is the hottest paprika.

Paprika

Peel/Zest—All outer peel of citrus fruits, also called zest, is used as an enhancer in stir-fries, stews, soups, sauces, and meat dishes. The rind of any citrus is a great source of antioxidants.

Peppercorns—Pepper adds a pungent, bold flavor to almost any dish.

Peppercorns

 Black—Pure black peppercorns imported from the Spice Islands of the South Pacific.

 Green—Native to India. The full, robust flavor is preferred by many for fish, seafood, and poultry.

 Pink—Actually a small exotic berry from the Reunion Islands. The sweet, delicate flavor and beautiful color will enhance any dish.

 Tellicherry—These peppercorns, grown on the Malabar Coast of India, have an aromatic flavor less bold than other black peppers.

 White—Premium Indonesian white peppercorns have a rich "sophisticated" flavor.

 Piri Piri— "Piri-piri" means "pepper-pepper" in the African language Swahili. It is a small-podded hot pepper brought to Portugal by Columbus. Used ground or as a powder, it is the main ingredient in the Piri-Piri hot sauce. Heat-index 8.

Poppy Seed

Poppy Seed—The slate-blue seeds are widely used in the Middle East, India, and Europe for both cooking and baking. Can be used as a garnish for breads, rolls, pastries, and cakes. Before using in a recipe, you can toast the seeds to increase the flavor.

Red Pepper Flakes—Red chili pepper flakes are used in soups, stews, and sauces. The bright red flakes are ideal to use as a garnish on pizzas, pastas, and Mexican dishes. Heat-index 6.

Red Pepper Flakes

Rosemary, dried—Rosemary does not lose its flavor even after being cooked for a long time, as many other leaves do. Use with fish, meat (especially poultry), vegetables, and potatoes. Also available ground.

Rosemary, dried

Saffron—The dark orange stigmata, called threads, have a rich, briny flavor. Saffron imparts a special pungent flavor to fish dishes, stews, paella and much more. Soak or infuse saffron threads before adding to a recipe.

Saffron

Salt—(sodium chloride) comes from salt mines, deposits of dried salt lakes, and ocean coastlines all over the world. Sea salt is the result of the evaporation of sea water, which is a costly process. Chefs all over the world praise the marvelous qualities of sea salt for its delicate flavor addition. There is a wide variety of salts available:

 Black Sea Salt—Black Sea Salt is a deeply fragrant salt from Pakistan, also known as Sanchal, used in many Asian dishes.

 Fleur de Sel—This French, low sodium sea salt, also known as the caviar-of-salt, sprinkled sparingly on cooked food is the "finishing touch." This salt is low in sodium and high in calcium.

Sea Salt, Black

 Hawaiian Red Sea Salt—The iron oxide, in the famous Hawaiian Red Clay, makes this salt the color of a burnt sienna. The large salt crystals, adds depth and complexity to its earthiness.

 Iodized Salt—A table salt with iodine added that regulates the thyroid.

Sea Salt, Hawaiian Red

Kosher Salt—Coarse-grained salt without additives; preferred by chefs in cooking, and used in Kosher Jewish cuisine.

Table Salt—A refined, fine-grained salt with additives, mostly used as a condiment.

Pure Refined Sea Salt—Finely ground pure sea salt has a great natural salt flavor; harvested by farmers in Brittany, France.

Sesame Seed—A popular ingredient in Asian cooking for over 2,000 years, now used around the world on bread, rolls, stir-fries, sushi, salads, chicken, fish, vegetables, rice, and noodle dishes. Sesame seed is used as a seasoning and for appearance.

Black—Black sesame seeds are stronger in aroma and flavor than white seeds, and are common in Asian and Middle Eastern dishes.

White—Sesame seeds are a delicious addition to many dishes.

Sumac—Often used instead of lemon juice, vinegar, or tamarind to create a "tangy" flavor.

Summer Savory—Savory is a delicious herb, due to its slight pepper-like flavor. In Bulgaria, summer savory is called *chubritsa*; in Germany, *Bohnenkraut*; and in Holland *bonen kruid*. These all translate to: used on any type of bean dish.

Szechwan Pepper—This is not really a peppercorn, but the berry of the Szechwan tree. It adds a spicy peppery flavor to your dishes.

Thyme, dried Spanish—Thyme is one of the strongest flavored herb; used for adding flavor to stir-fries, vegetables, soups, fish, meat, poultry, and eggs. Dried thyme is available as both leaves and powder.

Turbinado Sugar—Turbinado Sugar is made using 100 percent pure Hawaiian cane sugar from the first pressing of the sugar cane, which keeps the natural molasses in the crystals. It has a flavor that is sweet and rich.

Turmeric—This member of the ginger family has been used for over 2,000 years in Asia and the Middle East. It adds a warm, mild aroma, and a yellow color to foods. Available ground and in slices. The turmeric root slices have an aromatic and spicy fragrance. Recent research indicates that turmeric can be helpful in the prevention of Alzheimer's disease.

Vanilla Bean—Vanilla beans have a rich flavor and pure aroma. Store vanilla beans in a cool dark location and never freeze the beans. Slice the beans open and scrape the brown beans out of the skin. Use half a bean for one teaspoon of extract and one full bean when the recipe calls for one tablespoon.

Wasabi—This green, powdered horseradish is a powerful, nose-tingling condiment made from a knobby green root. Used in sushi, mixed with soy sauce for a dip,it is a delicious addition to stir-fries, Asian salads, and prepared vegetables.

Kosher Salt

Sumac

Summer Savory

Turbinado Sugar

Turmeric

Vanilla Beans

Wasabi

21

Spice Up Your Dishes

This chart shows spices indigenous to world cuisines.

Spice	African	Cajun	Caribbean	Chinese	Creole	Dutch	French	German	Greek	Hawaiian	Hungarian	Italian	Indian	Indonesian	Japanese	Korean	Magreb	Malaysian	Mediterranean	Mexican	SW American	Portuguese	Scandinavian	South American	Spanish	Thai	Turkish	Vietnamese
Allspice			√			√																		√			√	
Anise Star							√		√				√		√	√				√								√
Arrowroot																												
Basil	√	√	√	√	√	√	√		√	√	√	√			√	√	√	√				√			√	√		√
Caraway Seeds			√			√	√	√		√	√		√		√	√	√	√	√	√	√	√						
Cardamom				√							√		√				√										√	
Cayenne Pepper	√	√	√		√						√								√	√	√							
Chili Powders	√	√	√		√									√		√	√	√		√	√	√		√	√	√		√
Chinese 5-Spice				√										√														
Chives	√	√	√				√			√	√	√					√			√							√	√
Cilantro	√	√	√	√	√					√			√	√	√	√	√	√		√	√	√		√	√	√		√
Cinnamon				√				√	√		√	√					√			√				√	√		√	
Cloves	√					√	√		√			√							√					√	√		√	
Coriander			√	√									√	√			√			√	√				√	√		
Cumin	√		√		√						√		√	√			√			√	√							
Curry Powder			√										√	√												√		
Dill						√	√	√			√		√				√						√					
Epazote																				√	√			√				
Fenugreek							√						√				√	√						√				
Flax Seed													√										√					
Galangal Root														√	√			√										
Garlic	√	√	√	√			√		√	√		√		√	√	√	√	√	√	√		√		√	√	√	√	√
Ginger			√	√						√				√	√	√		√								√	√	√
Hyssop Herb								√		√							√											
Jalapeño																				√	√			√				
Mace, dried			√			√	√			√		√					√			√								
Nutmeg			√			√													√								√	
Oregano	√	√	√				√		√	√	√	√		√			√		√	√	√	√		√	√	√	√	√
Paprika		√									√														√			
Parsley			√	√	√		√		√	√	√						√	√	√			√			√			
Peel/Zest	√		√				√		√		√			√			√		√								√	
Pepper			√		√	√	√	√	√	√	√	√					√		√			√	√		√			
Piri Piri																	√					√						
Poppy Seed						√		√				√					√		√						√		√	
Red Pepper	√	√	√	√	√						√			√		√	√	√		√	√	√		√			√	√
Rosemary	√						√		√		√	√					√		√			√			√			
Saffron							√						√				√		√						√			
(Pure Sea) Salt		√	√		√		√			√							√		√				√	√				
Sesame Seed				√									√	√	√	√			√							√	√	
Sumac													√	√														
Summer Savory		√			√	√	√	√			√	√					√		√					√				
Szechwan Pepper				√										√														
Thyme	√	√	√		√	√	√	√	√	√	√	√					√			√							√	
Sugar						√					√			√	√	√										√	√	
Turmeric			√								√		√	√			√	√						√	√	√		√
Vanilla Bean			√		√	√														√	√						√	
Wasabi															√													

Herbs of the World

This chart shows fresh herbs indigenous to different cuisines. In infusion-cooking, you can be creative and dare to pick an herb non-indigenous, like basil in ice cream, green tea in marinades, etc. Just try it!

	African	Cajun	Caribbean	Chinese	Creole	Dutch	French	German	Greek	Hawaiian	Hungarian	Italian	Indian	Indonesian	Japanese	Korean	Magreb	Malaysian	Mediterranean	Mexican	SW American	Portuguese	Scandinavian	South American	Spanish	Thai	Turkish	Vietnamese
Basil	√	√	√	√	√	√	√		√		√	√	√		√	√	√	√					√			√		√
Bay Leaves	√		√	√	√	√	√				√	√		√					√	√								
Caraway			√			√	√	√			√		√		√	√	√				√		√					
Chervil			√	√	√		√	√	√		√	√				√						√		√				
Chives	√	√	√	√	√	√	√					√			√	√												
Chinese Chives				√										√	√	√										√		√
Cilantro	√	√	√	√	√									√	√	√	√			√	√			√	√	√	√	√
Dill						√	√	√			√	√				√							√					
Fennel			√				√	√				√											√					
Garlic	√	√	√	√	√		√		√	√	√	√	√		√	√	√	√	√	√	√			√	√	√	√	√
Ginger			√	√	√							√		√	√	√	√	√								√		√
Horseradish					√	√	√																√					
Kaffir Lime Leaf			√								√			√	√		√	√								√		√
Lavender		√					√		√		√	√					√		√				√					
Lemon Grass			√								√			√	√	√	√	√								√		√
Lemon Verbena	√				√										√		√	√	√									
Marjoram	√					√		√	√		√	√				√			√					√			√	
Mint	√	√				√	√		√		√	√	√		√	√	√		√					√		√	√	√
Oregano	√	√	√				√		√		√	√		√		√		√	√	√	√			√	√	√	√	√
Parsley			√	√	√		√		√			√				√	√		√			√		√				
Rosemary	√						√		√			√							√	√	√	√			√			
Sage	√			√			√		√			√							√								√	
Savory		√					√				√	√				√								√				
Tarragon							√				√	√				√		√				√		√	√		√	
Thyme	√	√	√		√	√	√	√	√		√	√		√						√							√	

Condiments of the World

	African	Cajun	Caribbean	Chinese	Creole	Dutch	French	German	Greek	Hawaiian	Hungarian	Italian	Indian	Indonesian	Japanese	Korean	Magreb	Malaysian	Mediterranean	Mexican	S-W American	Portuguese	Scandinavian	South American	Spanish	Thai	Turkish	Vietnamese
Citrus Juice	√	√	√		√		√		√	√	√	√		√		√	√	√		√		√	√		√	√	√	√
Coconut Milk	√		√		√		√		√	√			√	√		√	√		√			√			√	√		√
Fish Sauce				√					√		√	√	√	√	√		√		√							√		√
Hoisin				√					√						√	√		√								√		√
Honey	√		√	√	√	√	√		√	√	√			√		√	√		√		√	√		√	√		√	
Hot Sauce	√	√	√	√	√	√			√			√		√		√		√		√	√	√		√		√		√
Ketjap			√						√				√	√	√	√		√								√		√
Liqueur		√	√		√	√	√	√	√		√				√		√	√		√	√	√	√	√				
Mirin															√	√		√								√		√
Mustard		√	√		√	√	√				√					√	√		√			√	√					
Oyster Sauce				√					√				√	√	√	√		√								√		√
Sake									√						√													
Sambal			√		√				√				√	√		√		√								√		√
Soy Sauce			√						√				√	√	√											√		√
Wine		√			√		√		√		√	√			√	√	√	√				√		√	√			

Fruits of the World

Apple-Banana

Champagne Grapes

Currants

Kumquats

Rambutan

Green & Golden Kiwi

Pomegranate

Fruit is a gift of "Mother Nature" that is as old as mankind. Apples were a favorite fruit of the ancient Greeks and Romans, and evidence shows that they have been around for at least 750,000 years! Most fruits are fat-free, sodium-free, cholesterol-free, loaded with vitamins, minerals, and are great sources of fiber.

Fruit can be used in stir-fries, desserts, salads, salsas, or eaten "as-is" with or without the skin. The zest of fruits such as Buddha's hand and citrus fruits are great flavoring agents for salads, sauces, and stir-fries. Fresh fruit is widely available because the fruit-producing countries have different harvest times.

Take a look at the huge list of beautifully colored, deliciously flavored fruits available: apricots, apples, atemoya, Asian pears, avocados, bananas, blackberries, blueberries, breadfruits, cactus pears, currants, cherries, chirimoyas, dates, durians, figs, gooseberries, grapes, grapefruits, guava, jack fruits, kiwis, lemons, limes, kumquats, lychees, mandarins, mangoes, mangosteen, melons, nectarines, oranges, papaya, passion fruits, peaches, pears, persimmons, pineapples, plums/prunes, pomegranates, rambutan, raspberries, sharon fruits, soursop fruits, strawberries, tangerines, ugli fruits, and watermelons.

Many of our recipes are prepared with fresh fruits. Try them out, and enjoy the natural sweetness of honey melon, the tanginess of a kumquat, or the crisp freshness of an apple—just to name a few.

Kumquats—A small fruit with an edible, thick, sweet skin and flesh with a tart pulp. The small evergreen shrub is native to China and Indochina and is extensively cultivated in Japan, Florida, and California. They are approximately the size of a plum. Kumquats are available preserved in syrup, used in a wide variety of dishes, and eaten as dessert.

Pomegranate—The pomegranate is one of the earliest cultivated fruits. Historical evidence suggests that man first began planting pomegranate trees sometime between 4,000 B.C. and 3,000 B.C. Throughout history, this richly-colored and delicious fruit has been revered as a symbol of health, fertility, and rebirth. Some cultures also believed it held profound and mystical healing powers. Still others chose to use it in more practical ways as a dye or decoration. The pomegranate tree, to which it was bound, represented eternal life.

The juice from pomegranates is one of nature's most powerful antioxidants. Pomegranate juice has more polyphenol antioxidants than any other juice. For more information about the incredibly refreshing pomegranate, go to www.pomwonderful.com.

Vegetables of the World

"Mother Nature" has a huge assortment of vegetables that can be used in stir-fries, salads, and soups. To make it easier, we have divided them in two groups: hard and soft veggies. The cooking time and temperature for the two groups are different. Hard veggies need more time to cook. Be careful not to overcook, or the texture will turn to mush. Soft veggies need less time and a lower temperature, so they will not wilt and lose their flavor and health benefits.

Soft Vegetables—artichoke hearts, Azuki beans*, bean sprouts, beets***, Belgium endive, black beans*, chickpeas*, corn, cucumber, eggplant (Brazilian, Italian, Japanese, purple, Thai, white), fiddlehead fern, kidney beans*, legumes**, lentils**, Lima beans*, mushrooms, Napa cabbage, pinto beans*, pole beans*, Savoy cabbage, soy beans, spinach, squash, and tomato.

IMPORTANT! NEVER re-heat dark greens, especially spinach. Cook quickly and serve immediately.

Hard Vegetables—asparagus, bell pepper, bok choy, broccoli, broccoli raab, brussels sprouts, cabbage (Chinese, red, etc.), carrots, celery, celeriac, choy sum, collard greens, cranberry beans, daikon, fava beans, fennel bulb, green beans, haricot verts, jicama, kale, kohlrabi, long beans, onion, peas, potato, radishes, seeds, snow peas, sugar snap peas, and yellow wax beans.

All vegetables are a great source of a wide variety of nutrients and flavors—and possibilities to be adventurous. When selecting, only pick the fresh, firm, and brightly colored looking vegetables with a pleasant aroma. Avoid any vegetables with brown spots, a musty smell, or those that look soggy or wilted. Store in a vacuum-sealed bag or storage container for as long as a few days in the refrigerator.

Cutting vegetables for later use (3–4 days in refrigerator) is possible if you can vacuum-seal them. Otherwise, fresh is always good! Here are a few examples that taste great in most every stir-fry:

Broccoli Raab—also called rapini. Used in stir-fries, steamed, sautéed, and boiled for side dishes, soups, and stews because of its slightly bitter flavor. To decrease the intensity of the flavor, blanch in salted water. Pick broccoli raab that is firm and bright green. Rinse it, shake off water, and cut off the bottom part of the stems. Available in all seasons, but its prime time is fall to spring.

Choy Sum—Choy sum are bright green leafy vegetables. The name means "vegetable hearts," and they are also known as bok choy sum or Chinese flowering cabbage. Used in stir-fries, great with a little ginger, garlic, and scallions. Blanching in salted water decreases the bitterness.

Kohlrabi—This root vegetable, also called turnip cabbage, is a family member of the cabbage. Trim off root and vinelike stems. Wash and peel, cut into cubes or into batonnets. Kohlrabi can be boiled, baked, steamed, and fried. Young kohlrabi can be used grated or diced small in salads.

Beans are cooked for ± 1 hour, or bought canned.
** Legumes like lentils are cooked for ± 3 minutes.*
*** Beets are baked for ± 1 hour, peeled, or bought pre-cooked.*

Cranberry Beans

Lima Beans

Napa Cabbage

Broccoli Raab

Bok Choy

Squash: Bitter Melon

Squash: Chayote

Mushrooms of the World

Mushrooms have a high water content, are low in calories, and contribute to our health because they are filled with vitamins and minerals. The flavor of mushrooms is earthy and intensifies during cooking because they have the ability to absorb the flavor of the cooking liquid. That's why you do not soak them in water. Brush or wipe them clean with a wet towel. Most mushrooms can be eaten raw (unless indicated otherwise) and are great grilled, roasted, sautéed, stir-fried, slowly braised, or used in soups, stews, and casseroles. Fresh thyme is a great flavor enhancer for mushrooms. Here are a few of the most commonly used:

Button Mushrooms—Firm, white mushrooms with a mild flavor. Available in all seasons.

Chanterelle Mushrooms—Chanterelle mushrooms have a light brown color with a nutty flavor. Cut off bottom of stems. Available in summer and fall.

Chinese Umbrella Mushrooms—Mild flavored mushroom, great for all kinds of stir-fries. Available canned or dried (soak before using).

Cremini Mushrooms—Cremini mushrooms have a cocoa brown color. They are also called Italian brown mushrooms. The distinct flavor of creminis intensifies during cooking. Available in all seasons.

Enoki Mushrooms—These off-white mushrooms look like sticks with little round buttons on top. Enoki have a fruity, crisp flavor. Cut off the base, which should look creamy, not brown or soggy.

Hen of the Woods Mushrooms—Hen of the Woods mushrooms are polypores, which means that more than one mushroom cap grows on each stem. The pearly white tops have brown ruffles. Pick only the mushrooms that are firm and do not smell musty. Available in late spring and late fall.

Morel Mushrooms—Found in the wild, but served with a very cultivated price tag ± $50.00 a pound. They have a smoky, earthy flavor, and an odd shape: like a honeycomb-covered kidney. Morel mushrooms should not have any sour smell. Available from early spring till mid summer.

Oyster Mushrooms—Grown in the wild on trees. Their flavor is mild, and they have a wavy, overlapping look with a silky surface. Not advised to eat them raw. Available in all seasons.

Porcini Mushrooms—A rare mushroom in the same price range as morels and truffles. Porcini mushrooms have a very rich, buttery flavor. Available in spring and fall.

Portobello Mushrooms—Portobello mushrooms are great substitutes for meat recipes. They are large, ± 4 to 6 inches wide with a thick stem, topped by a dappled brown cap with dark brown gills.

Shiitake Mushrooms—Popular, due to their rich, garlic-pine flavor. Fresh shiitakes have a strong fragrance; if they are odorless, they are not fresh. Do not eat uncooked. Available in all seasons.

Wood Ear Mushrooms—Glossy brown to black with a mild flavor. The only mushroom you should soak; they expand to six times their size when soaked in hot water. Rinse thoroughly.

Cremini Mushroom

Chanterelle Mushroom, Red

Chinese Umbrella Mushroom

Oyster Mushroom

King Oyster Mushroom

Portobello Mushroom

Shiitake Mushroom

Onions of the World

Onions can be placed into two categories: green onions and dry onions. After cutting off the bottom root, green onions can be used from top to bottom. Dry onions have been cured, so their dry skin has to be peeled off. Onions can be chopped, minced, diced, julienned, and quartered to place on the grill. They are good for our health and have bold flavors. Pick "heavy," firm onions without soft spots or growing sprouts. They can be used raw, grilled, caramelized, cooked in soups, sauces, casseroles, salads, and of course in stir-fries.

Boiling Onions—Boiling onions are white, small and round, about 1" to 1½" in diameter. Their flavor is mild. Pick "heavy" onions: when onions get older, they dry out and loose weight. Submerge in boiling water for ± 30 seconds, shock in cold water, and push out of their skin.

Boiling Onions

Green Onions, Spring Onions, Scallions—These onions have long, straight, dark green leaves, and a white root that has not completely matured into a bulb. When the green onions have a flat base, they are called scallions. Their flavor is milder than green onions with a round base. Both are delicious in salads, sliced very thin in brothy soups, and in stir-fries. Look for bright, fresh-looking leaves. Cut off the root part, cut in thin slices, or 2" long strips.

Scallion or Spring Onions

Japanese Onions—Common in Asia, especially Japan, and also grown on the Hawaiian island Oahu. These onions are longer than leeks, but slightly thinner. The flavor is crisp and bold, and their color is bright. Great for stir-fries, in soups and stews. Where grown, they are available all seasons.

Japanese Onion

Knob Onions—Also called bald onion and Florida sweet onion. They have thick green stems, like leeks, and rounded white bulbs. Look for bright, fresh-looking and firm leaves. Cut off roots and cut as desired. Available in all seasons; at their best in late spring and summer.

Knob onion

Leeks—Leeks are related to onions and garlic, which explains their sweet flavor. Only the white and very pale green parts of a leek should be eaten. Rinse thoroughly.

Leek

Pearl Onion—Pearl onions are not more than 1" in diameter. Their flavor is sweet and pungent. Pick firm onions that have dry papery skin. Avoid soft onions with green or black blemishes.

Shallots—A member of the onion family, but they look like garlic cloves packed separately. Their color is layered from purple on the outside to green and then white on the inside. Slice off the roots and remove skin, then chop or mince. Used in salads, dressings, and meat dishes.

Shallot, White, Yellow & Red Onion

Spanish Onion—Grown and consumed all over the world as flavor-enhancers. Their large, yellow bulbs have a mild, non-overpowering flavor, but are not as sweet as Vidalia or Maui onions.

Vidalia® or Sweet Onion—A fairly new, hybrid of sweet onions. Vidalia® (Vie-DALE-yah) is a mild and creamy onion, that can only carry the name Vidalia® if grown in 19 specified Georgia counties. They are highly perishable, due to their high moisture content.

Vidalia® Onion

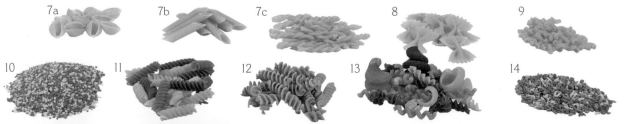

1   2   3   4   5   6

Pasta & Noodles of the World

Pasta can be divided into two kinds: dry pasta (pasta secca) and fresh pasta (pasta fresca). Fresh pasta has been a main staple in many Mediterranean cuisines since the times of the Romans, the Greeks, and the Arabs. Dry pasta, as we show a few examples here, began in Italy and conquered the whole world. There is a pasta for every taste and desire, even for people who follow a low-carb regimen. The time to cook pasta ranges from 2 minutes for thin, small-sized to 13 minutes for thick, large-sized pasta.

1. **Angel Hair**—A very thin pasta, available in 100 percent semolina and whole wheat. Cooks in only 2 minutes.

2. **Fusilli**—A macaroni product made of 100 percent pure Italian durum wheat semolina. These are fun pasta sticks ready in 8 minutes.

3. **Linguine**—A medium-size, flat pasta that holds up well with bold, tomato based recipes. Cooks in ± 12 minutes.

4. **Capellini**—A little thicker than angel hair, thinner than spaghetti, but as delicious as all the others. Cooks in 4-5 minutes.

5. **Whole Wheat Spaghetti**—Made from wheat germ and bran fiber, which provides a nutritious and delicious pasta, ready in less than 10 minutes.

6. **Spaghetti**—A round, medium thick pasta, which is the most familiar of all in the pasta family. Cooks in ± 11 minutes.

7. **Trio Italiano**—a: Rotini, b: Mostaccioli, c: Shells, all in one package full of the delicious flavor of 100 percent durum semolina, but shaped in their own way. Cooks in ± 11 minutes.

8. **Farfalle**—A bow-tie pasta, made from 100 percent Italian durum semolina. Available in different sizes. Cooks in ± 10 minutes.

9. **Elbow Macaroni**—The original macaroni made from 100 percent semolina. Cooks in ± 7 minutes.

10. **Tricolor Couscous**—Couscous is the main staple of Magreb (North-African) cuisine. The small grain-pellet can be made from wheat semolina, barley, corn, rice, and the most common: buckwheat semolina. Israeli couscous has a larger grain. Boxed couscous is pre-cooked and great for soups. Bulk couscous has to be steamed, great for salads and to serve with stir-fries.

11. **Tricolore Rotini**—Can't make up your mind which color pasta to pick? Take all 3: plain, orange, and green.

12. **Kamut Spirals**—A rotini made from 100 percent whole grain kamut. Organic, low in total fat, low in cholesterol. Cooks in ± 8 minutes.

13. **Carnival in Venice**—The best way to describe this pasta: multi-colored, multi-shaped: twists, curly, and little turrets of playful pasta. Cooks in ± 10 minutes.

14. **Vegetable Alphabet Pasta**—Spell your name with this healthy pasta made from golden amber durum wheat. Cooks in ± 4 minutes.

7a   7b   7c   8   9

10   11   12   13   14

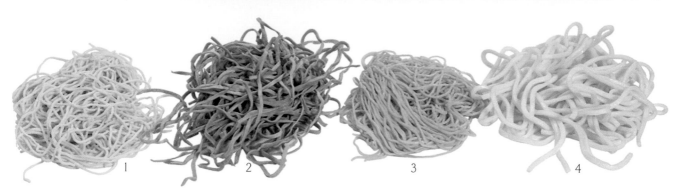

1   2   3   4

Noodles come in a wide variety of shapes, colors, and flavors. These are a few examples. The first four are already cooked. Noodles 4–10 are less perishable because they are dried:

1. Shanghai—A round, bleached, wheat flour noodle. Prep: dip in boiling water for 2 minutes. Drain, serve, or add to stir-fry pan. Available in large or small bundles.

2. Vegetable Noodle—A flat, green noodle made of flour, water, and spinach/broccoli/celery powder. Prep: dip noodles in boiling water for 20 seconds. Drain and serve or add to stir-fry pan.

3. Cooked Noodle—A round, yellow noodle made of flour, water, and eggs. Prep: can be served cold or added to stir-fry pan.

4. Udon Japanese-Style Noodle—A thick, white noodle made of flour, water, and a little corn oil. Prep: can be added to a soup or the stir-fry pan full with flavorful veggies and/or meats.

5. Vermicelli Noodle—A thin, white cellophane noodle, made of the finest starch of mung beans, peas, mixed beans, potato, and maize. Place of origin is China, but available in any Asian store. Prep: soak in water for 2 minutes, drain, and add to stir-fry pan.

6. Lo Mein Noodle—A thin, yellow noodle made from wheat flour and eggs. Prep: place noodle in boiling water for 1 minute, drain and add to stir-fry pan.

7. Oriental-style Noodle—A thin, grayish cellophane noodle indigenous to Korea. Made from sweet potato flour and water. Prep: boil for ± 5 minutes, drain, serve or add to stir-fry pan.

8. Egg Noodle—A noodle made of durian flour and egg. Prep: boil for ± 5–7 minutes, drain, serve or add to stir-fry pan.

9. Chinese-style Noodle—A flat, yellow noodle rolled into a "bird's nest." Prep: boil for ± 5 minutes, drain, and add to pan.

10. Pad Thai Noodle—A flat, rice sticky noodle used in the traditional Thai dish. Prep: soak in hot water for 3 minutes, drain and add to stir-fry pan.

5   6   7   8   9   10

Rice of the World

Rice is a great source of vitamins, fiber, manganese, and phosphorus. Choose a low-glycemic rice with great flavors, like a brown rice, multi-grain, or even a Chinese black rice. Lotus Foods is one of the companies specializing in rice from all over the world. A rice cooker is an ideal tool to cook rice fast and easy. For more information go to www.lotusfoods.com.

Bhutanese Red Rice—Grows at 8,000 feet in the Himalayan Kingdom of Bhutan. Irrigated with 1,000-year-old glacier water rich in trace minerals, this premium heirloom rice is distinguished by its complex nutty flavor and beautiful russet color. It is the perfect complement to full-flavored vegetables, fish, fowl, and game. A great rice served steamed or in stir-fries.

Calriso Mediterranean Rice—If you find 40 degrees north latitude on your globe and trace its path around the world, this parallel will pass through the great rice growing regions of Italy, Spain, Turkey, northern China, and Japan, and across the Pacific to fall in the Sacramento Valley of California. As a product of the careful crossing of Italian and Californian rice varieties, Calriso is the first Mediterranean rice born in the New World. Rich in starch, which releases during cooking and stirring, Calriso makes a creamy risotto and a perfect paella. It is also freshly milled to arrive in your kitchen moist and full of flavor.

Carnaroli Rice—Originating from Italy's famous Poe River Valley, the premium Carnaroli is now estate grown at the foot of the Andes Mountains in the fertile valleys of central Argentina. Prized by chefs throughout the world for its bold white kernel, uniform starch release, and resulting creamy texture, Carnaroli is the preferred rice for world-class risotto.

Jasmine Rice—Considered the premium rice of choice in Thailand. Also referred to as "fragrant rice" due to its floral aroma and flavor. I. G. Raun, a third generation rice farmer, cultivates the Lotus Foods Organic Jasmine Rice in the fertile plains of the Texas Gulf Coast. Unlike most brown rice that becomes chewy, this long-grain brown rice is distinguished by its moist and tender texture.

Kalijira Rice—Considered the premium rice of Bangladesh; known as the "Prince of Rice" for its delicious and delicate flavor. Like baby-basmati, this aromatic tiny rice is easy and quick to cook (± 10 minutes).

Forbidden Rice—Product of China: legend tells us that this ancient grain was once only grown exclusively for the emperors of China to enrich their health and ensure longevity. Today, this medium-size Chinese black rice can be enjoyed every day and is prized for its fragrant aroma, nutty taste, soft texture, and beautiful rich, deep purple color. High in nutritional and medicinal value, Forbidden Rice is unlike other black rice. It is not glutinous or rough, and cooks in only 30 minutes.

Soy, a Healthy Protein Source

CHD is the most common most serious form of cardiovascular disease. It is the number one cause of death in the United States. Despite the decline in deaths from CHD over the past thirty years, this disease still causes more than 500,000 deaths annually and contributes to another 250,000 deaths. Total high blood cholesterol and high low-density lipoprotein (LDL) cholesterol levels are proven risk factors for CHD.

In proposing this health claim, the FDA concluded that foods containing protein from the soybean as part of a diet low in saturated fat and cholesterol may reduce the risk of heart disease by lowering total blood cholesterol and LDL-cholesterol. Studies show 25 grams of soy protein per day has a cholesterol-lowering effect. Therefore, for a food to qualify for the health claim, each serving of food must contain at least 6.25 grams of soy protein, or one-fourth of the 25-gram amount shown to have a cholesterol-lowering effect. Advice: 1–2 servings of soy foods a day. Here are a few examples of soy products:

Bean Sprouts—Sprouts of the soybean are great sources of Vitamins A, B, C, and E, calcium, iron, magnesium, phosphorus, amino acids, and protein.

Edamame—This green soybean is harvested at the peak of ripening, just before it hardens. For freshness and flavor, they are parboiled and quickly frozen. Consumed as a snack (boiled in lightly salted water then pushed from the pod into the mouth), or as a vegetable in soups and stir-fries.

Miso—Thick paste of fermented soybeans, varying in flavor: pale yellow is mild, red is salty, and brown is stronger flavored.

Soy Flour—A multi-purpose flour made by grinding roasted soybeans into a fine powder. The flour adds protein and moisture, so it can be used as an egg substitute in baked products.

Soy milk—A soy beverage produced by grinding dehulled soybeans and water to form a milk-like liquid. A good milk substitute for lactose-intolerant people. Available fortified with calcium, plain, or flavored; can be used in recipes that call for cream or half & half.

Soy Nuts—These "nuts" are soybeans soaked for more than 8 hours, then roasted in the oven with a pinch of salt. A handful of nuts is a healthy way to satisfy your cravings.

Soy Sauce—A dark sauce made of fermented soy beans. The low-sodium version is ideal to season stir-fries, soups, and marinades.

Tempeh—A favorite food and protein source in Indonesia for several hundred years. Made from whole, cooked soybeans pressed into a chewy cookie and used as a meat substitute.

Tofu—Tofu is soybean curd, made by treating heated soy milk with a coagulant to produce curds, pressed to different firmness: soft for soups, regular and firm for sautéing and stir-fries.

soy sauce

tofu

soy milk

soy nuts

bean sprouts

edamame

edamame

Beef

Choose lean beef with a little marbling and cut away excess fat: tenderloin, filet mignon, pre-cut stir-fry beef, top sirloin, and ground beef. Buffalo steak and venison are also great meats for stir-fry.

Bo Xao Ot Stir-Fry

shopping/to-do list

8–10 oz. lean beef, bite-size pieces
½ each green bell pepper, orange bell pepper, and yellow bell pepper, cut into thin strips
½ T hot pepper, finely chopped
1 T shallots, minced
2 T lemon grass, chopped

Marinade:

1 T each ginger and garlic
⅓ cup low sodium soy sauce
1 T star anise, ground
1 T coriander
1 cup rice noodles, soaked

Serves 2 Dinners/3 Lunches

PREP 1:10   COOK 0:06

Bo Xao Ot is a traditional dish from Vietnam: marinated beef, stir-fried with bell peppers, served over a bed of cellophane noodles. We added a few more colors, but the traditional flavors are still as delicious as ever.

1   Cut ingredients into desired sizes. Mix marinade, pour over meat, and let marinate for at least 1 hour.

2   Add a little oil or cooking spray of your choice to the pan. Heat pan to 400°F/high heat.

3   Add meat. Stir around for 2 minutes to brown on all sides. Add bell pepper, shallot, and hot pepper. Stir around for 2 minutes.

4   Add lemongrass. Stir around for an additional minute. Serve over rice noodles, soaked in hot water.

"Climbing Ants" Stir-Fry

shopping/to-do list

8–12 oz. coarse ground beef
1 cup choy of choice, sliced
1 cup leek
1 cup celery, sliced
1 red hot pepper, chopped
1 T garlic, minced
1 T fresh grated ginger
1/3 cup beef or veggie stock
1 T Szechwan pepper
1 T low sodium soy sauce
2 cups cooked mihoen noodles
Serve with hot sauce on the side.

Serves 2 Dinners/3 Lunches

0:09 PREP   0:06 COOK

This spicy Chinese recipe is prepared with coarse ground meat and served with mihoen. The Chinese call it "Ants Climbing in the Trees" because the meatpieces resemble ants.

1 Cut ingredients into desired sizes.

2 Add a little oil or cooking spray of your choice to the pan. Heat pan to 400°F/high heat.

3 Add ground beef. Stir around for 2 minutes to loosen and brown the beef.

4 Add choy, leek, celery, hot pepper, garlic, and ginger. Stir around for 2 minutes.

5 Add stock, Szechwan pepper, low sodium soy sauce and noodles. Stir around for additional minute. Serve with hot sauce on the side.

"Chud" Stir-Fry

shopping/to-do list

8–12 oz. lean beef, cut into ½" strips
1 cup sugar snap peas, sliced
1 cup carrots, sliced
1 small onion, sliced thin
1 green bell pepper, chopped
1 T garlic, minced
1 T fresh grated ginger
1 T red crushed pepper
1 T low sodium soy sauce
1 cup stock of choice: beef, veggie

Serves 2 Dinners/3 Lunches

PREP 0:10   COOK 0:06

Chud is a Thai clear soup, in which you can use any kind of ingredient available. Our version is prepared with beef slices, but you can replace that with chicken, pork, veal, or tofu.

1   Cut ingredients into desired sizes.

2   Add a little oil or cooking spray of your choice to the pan. Heat pan to 400°F/high heat.

3   Add beef. Stir around for 2 minutes to brown on all sides.

4   Add peas, carrots, onion, bell pepper, garlic, and ginger. Stir around for 2 minutes.

5   Add red crushed pepper, low sodium soy sauce, and stock. Let come to a boil for additional 1 minute.

Beef Criolla Stir-Fry

shopping/to-do list

8–12 oz. beef, cut into ½" strips
1 cup winter squash, diced small
1 cup corn kernels
½ cup peaches, sliced
1 T cilantro leaves
½ T hot sauce
salt & pepper to taste
Serve over rice or mashed potatoes.

Serves 2 Dinners/3 Lunches

PREP   COOK

Stir-fry of three yellow/orange-colored vegetables and fruits: yellow winter squash, corn, and peaches. It can be served in the squash shell.

1 Cut ingredients into desired sizes.

2 Add a little oil or cooking spray of your choice to the pan. Heat pan to 400°F/high heat.

3 Add beef. Stir around for 2 minutes to brown on all sides.

4 Add squash and corn. Stir around for 2 minutes.

5 Add peaches, cilantro, hot sauce, salt, and pepper to taste. Stir around for an additional minute. Serve over rice or mashed potatoes.

Argentina Carbonada Stir-Fry

shopping/to-do list

8–12 oz. beef cut into ½" strips
1 apple, cored and sliced
1 pear, cored and medium diced
2 tomatoes, medium diced
1 onion, chopped
2 medium size potatoes, peeled,
and shredded
salt & pepper to taste

Serves 2 Dinners/3 Lunches

PREP   COOK

*Argentina is a country known for great beef,
and this popular beef dish, prepared with a
fast and easy stir-fry technique indigenous
to China, is a delicious infusion of cuisines.*

1   Cut ingredients into desired sizes.

2   Add a little oil or cooking spray of your choice to the pan. Heat pan to
400°F/high heat.

3   Add beef. Stir around for 2 minutes to brown on all sides.

4   Add apple, pear, tomatoes, onion, and potato. Stir around for
2 minutes.

5   Add salt and pepper to taste. Stir around for additional minute.

Salami & Tomato Stir-Fry

shopping/to-do list

1 onion, diced
½ bell pepper, sliced thin
3 x ¼" thick salami sliced, cubed
1 tomato, diced
1 T garlic, minced
1 T tomato paste
1 T paprika powder
2 T oregano
salt & pepper to taste
Can be served over pasta of choice.

Serves 2 Dinners/3 Lunches

PREP   COOK

Deli cold cuts are considered an easy alternative to meat, especially because the stir-fry time can be cut in half. The substitutes for salami are unlimited and all delicious, but do choose low-sodium cuts.

1   Cut ingredients into desired sizes.

2   Add a little oil or cooking spray of your choice to the pan. Heat pan to 400°F/high heat.

3   Add onion and bell pepper. Stir around for 2 minutes.

4   Add salami, tomato, garlic, tomato paste, paprika powder, and oregano. Stir around for 2 minutes.

5   Add salt and pepper to taste. Stir around for additional minute. Serve over pasta of choice.

Papaya & Beef Stir-Fry

shopping/to do list

8–12 oz. lean beef, sliced thin
1 cup papaya, diced small
1 chili, chopped finely
1 T coriander
1 T ginger, fresh grated
1 t nutmeg
1 t cayenne
⅓ cup coconut cream
salt & pepper to taste
Serve over rice or potatoes of choice. Garnish
with grated coconut.

Serves 2 Dinners/3 Lunches

PREP 0:07   COOK 0:06

*The sweet flavor of the papaya fruit infuses
very well with the bold beef flavor. Other
fruits can be added or used as substitutes.*

1 Cut ingredients into desired sizes.

2 Add a little oil or cooking spray of your choice to the pan. Heat pan to
400°F/high heat.

3 Add beef. Stir around for 2 minutes to brown on all sides.

4 Add papaya, chiles, coriander, ginger, nutmeg, cayenne, and coconut
cream. Stir around for 2 minutes.

5 Season with salt and pepper to taste. Stir around for an additional minute.
Serve over rice or potatoes of choice, garnish with grated coconut.

Spanish Beef Stir-Fry

Serves 2 Dinners/3 Lunches

PREP   COOK

The running bulls of Pamplona are famous all over the world. Beef is used in pies, croquettes, and ground in stews and soups. This meatball stir-fry is easy, fast, and delicious. Check Chapter 11 to see how fast and easy it is to make meatballs.

1 Cut ingredients into desired sizes.

2 Add a little oil or cooking spray of your choice to the pan. Heat pan to 400°F/high heat.

3 Add ground beef. Stir around for 2 minutes to loosen up and brown.

4 Add onion, bell peppers, chickpeas, garlic, cumin, paprika powder, and olives. Stir around for 2 minutes.

5 Add salt and pepper to taste. Stir around for an additional minute. Serve with yellow rice.

Asian Sweet & Sour Stir-Fry

shopping/to-do list

8–12 oz. lean beef, cut into ½" strips
1 cup bok choy, sliced
½ cup celery, sliced
1 cup soy bean sprouts
1 small onion, sliced thin
1 green hot pepper, chopped
1 T garlic, minced
1 T fresh grated ginger
1 T Szechwan pepper
1 T low sodium soy sauce

Serves 2 Dinners/3 Lunches

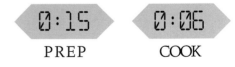

0:15
PREP

0:06
COOK

Sweet and sour reflects life: the good and the bad times, joy and sadness, rich and poor. A very down-to-earth view translated into a variety of recipes in Chinese cuisine.

1 Cut ingredients into desired sizes.

2 Add a little oil or cooking spray of your choice to the pan. Heat pan to 400°F/high heat.

3 Add beef. Stir around for 2 minutes to brown on all sides.

4 Add bok choy, celery, bean sprouts, onion, hot pepper, garlic, and ginger. Stir around for 2 minutes.

5 Add Szechwan pepper and low sodium soy sauce to taste. Stir around for additional minute.

Tangy Beef Stir-Fry

PREP   COOK

Citrus contains natural ingredients that have a tenderizing effect. When using a less lean cut of beef, marinating is the solution to make it more tender. Let it marinade for at least 2 hours. When using lean beef, the marinate can be used as the cooking liquid.

shopping/to-do list

8–12 oz. lean beef, thin sliced
1 small onion, diced
1 green bell pepper, sliced thin
½ each orange, lime, lemon
segments, zest reserved
1 t hot sauce
salt & pepper to taste

Marinade/Cooking Liquid:

1 cup orange/lime/lemon juice
1 t ginger, minced
1 t coriander
⅓ cup soy sauce
Serve with rice, couscous, or pasta.

1   Cut ingredients into desired sizes. Mix marinade ingredients, let meat marinate for ± 2 hours. Lean beef doesn't require marinating.

2   Add a little oil or cooking spray of your choice to the pan. Heat pan to 400°F/high heat.

3   Add beef, onion, and bell pepper. Stir around for 2 minutes to brown on all sides.

4   Add orange, lime, and lemon segments, cooking liquid (if not marinating), and hot sauce. Season with a little salt and pepper to taste. Stir around for an additional minute. Serve with rice, couscous, or pasta. Garnish with cilantro sprigs and a little zest.

Beef & Broccoli Stir-Fry

Serves 2 Dinners/3 Lunches

0:05 PREP **0:06** COOK

shopping/to-do list

8–12 oz. lean beef, bite-size pieces
1 cup broccoli florets
1 cup small cauliflower florets
1 onion, sliced thin
1 red (hot) pepper, chopped
½ cup miniature corn
1 T garlic, minced
½ cup cashew nuts
salt & pepper to taste
1 T low sodium soy sauce
Serve over rice or noodles of choice

A traditional stir-fry containing beef, veggies, peppers, and nuts served over noodles or rice is the main staple in many Asian households. It is delicious, quick to prepare, and healthy for the body and mind.

1 Cut ingredients into desired sizes.

2 Add a little oil or cooking spray of your choice to the pan. Heat pan to 400°F/high heat.

3 Add beef. Stir around for 2 minutes to brown on all sides.

4 Add broccoli, cauliflower, onion, red pepper, miniature corn, and garlic. Stir around for 2 minutes.

5 Add cashew nuts and season to taste. Stir around for an additional minute. Serve over rice of choice, see page 30.

Fish

2 Fish is a great source of protein and omega-3 fatty acids, which help fight cardiovascular diseases. Firm textured fish (mackerel, mahi-mahi, tilapia, tuna) are easier to use for stir-frying, but flaky textured (bass, orange roughy, salmon, white fish) and softer textured fish (bluefish, flounder, sole) are great to use, too.

Mediterranean Salmon Stir-Fry

shopping/to-do list

8–12 oz. salmon, cut into bite-size pieces
1 onion, sliced thin
1 T garlic
1 T capers
2 cups escarole
2 T cream or half & half
2 T pine nuts
⅓ cup white wine (optional)
1 T dill
sea salt & pepper to taste
Serve over linguine and garnish with dill.

Serves 2 Dinners/3 Lunches

0:10
PREP

0:06
COOK

Salmon is a beautifully colored, delicious fish popular all over the world. The flavor of salmon can be infused with all five flavor groups; this is a fish with unlimited seasoning opportunities.

1   Cut ingredients into desired sizes.

2   Add a little oil or cooking spray of your choice to the pan. Heat pan to 375° F/medium-high heat.

3   Add salmon. Stir around for 2 minutes.

4   Add onion, capers, and garlic. Stir around for 2 minutes.

5   Add escarole, sea salt, and pepper to taste. Finish with cream, wine, pine nuts, and dill. Stir around for an additional minute. Serve over linguine and garnish with dill.

Simply White Fish Stir-Fry

PREP   COOK

White is not an official color but the lack of color. This recipe of only white ingredients is not lacking anything. It is flavorful, and even though the ingredients are called white, they do have a little color.

shopping/to-do list

1 small white onion, sliced thin
8-10 oz. white fish of choice, cut into strips
1 t horseradish, minced
1 cup white mushrooms, sliced
1 T garlic, minced
1 cup white grapes, cut in halves
1 cup white wine
1 T white pepper
a pinch sea salt to taste
Serve over rice or mashed potatoes.

1. Cut ingredients into desired sizes.

2. Add a little oil or cooking spray of your choice to the pan. Heat pan to 375° F/medium-high heat.

3. Add onion. Stir around for a minute.

4. Add fish, horseradish, mushroom, and garlic. Stir around for 2 minutes.

5. Add grapes, wine, sea salt, and pepper to taste. Stir around for an additional minute. Serve over rice or mashed potatoes.

Halibut Stir-Fry

Serves 2 Dinners/3 Lunches

shopping/to do list

8–12 oz. halibut, cut into bite-size pieces
1 cup green beans, cut into 1" pieces
2 cup Napa cabbage, sliced
1 cup eggplant, diced small
1 T garlic
1 T chervil sprigs
salt & pepper
Serve with roasted potatoes
and garnished with chervil.

0:10
PREP

0:05
COOK

Fish is an ideal ingredient for stir-frying due to its short cooking time and its great health benefits, like omega-3, that help reduce cholesterol and lower high blood pressure.

1   Cut ingredients in desired sizes.

2   Add a little oil or cooking spray of your choice to the pan. Heat pan to 375° F/medium-high heat.

3   Add beans, stir around for 1 minute.

4   Add halibut, cabbage, eggplant, and garlic. Stir around for 2 minutes.

5   Add salt and pepper to taste. Stir around for an additional minute. Serve with roasted potatoes and garnish with chervil sprigs.

Catfish Stir-Fry

Serves 2 Dinners/3 Lunches

0:07	0:06
PREP	COOK

shopping/to do list

1 onion, chopped finely
1 green bell pepper, sliced thin
1 cup celery, sliced
1 lb. catfish filet, cut in bite-size pieces
1 T garlic, minced
1 t cajun seasoning, see Chapter 10
½ cup fresh basil, chiffonade
⅓ cup white wine.
Serve over rice of choice.

To the French, the seasoning trio of onion, celery, and carrots, sautéed in butter is "mirepoix." "Holy Trinity" is the Louisiana version: celery, onions, and green bell peppers used in Cajun and Creole cooking.

1   Cut all ingredients into described sizes.

2   Add a little oil or cooking spray of your choice to the pan. Heat pan to 375° F/medium-high heat.

3   Add onion, bell pepper, and celery. Stir around for 2 minutes.

4   Add fish, garlic, seasoning, and wine. Stir around for 2 minutes.

5   Serve over cooked rice of choice. Garnish with a basil chiffonade.

Thai Red Snapper Stir-Fry

Serves 2 Dinners/3 Lunches

0:12 PREP   0:06 COOK

The red snapper feeds on crustaceans and other fish, which gives its flesh a full-bodied flavor. In the United States, most red snappers are caught in the Florida Panhandle.

shopping/to-do list

8–12 oz. red snapper fillets, cut into
½" strips
1 cucumber, sliced
1 cup bean sprouts
1 small onion, sliced thin
1 green hot pepper, chopped
1 T garlic, minced
1 T fresh grated ginger
1 t cardamom
1 T cilantro chopped
Fish sauce, pepper, and hot sauce to taste
Serve over rice or noodles.

1   Cut ingredients into desired sizes.

2   Add a little oil or cooking spray of your choice to the pan. Heat pan to 375° F/medium-high heat.

3   Add fish and onion. Stir around for 2 minutes.

4   Add cucumber, bean sprouts, hot pepper, garlic, and ginger. Stir around for 2 minutes.

5   Add cardamom and season with fish sauce, pepper, and hot sauce to taste. Stir around for an additional minute. Serve over rice or noodles.

Cod Stir-Fry à la Normandy

Serves 2 Dinners/3 Lunches

PREP 0:15 **COOK** 0:06

The Vikings survived their long journeys due to dried cod, and nowadays cod is still a popular fish—dried or freshly caught. This recipe combines cod with fresh veggies and herbs.

shopping/to-do list

1 lb. cod, sliced into ½" strips
2 cups broccoli florets
1 eggplant, small cubed
2 tomatoes, small diced
2 T parsley, chopped
1 t lemon juice
sea salt & black pepper to taste
Served with roasted rosemary
potatoes.

1. Cut ingredients into the desired sizes.

2. Add a little oil or cooking spray of your choice to the pan. Heat pan to 375° F/medium-high heat.

3. Add cod and broccoli. Stir around for 2 minutes.

4. Add eggplant, tomato, and parsley. Stir around for 2 minutes.

5. Add lemon juice, sea salt, and pepper to taste. Stir around for an additional minute. Serve with roasted rosemary potatoes.

Bouillabaisse Stir-Fry

Serves 2 Dinners/3 Lunches

PREP   COOK

Bouillabaisse is a famous fishermen's stew indigenous to Marseille. Made here in the wok with a variety of local fish, shellfish, saffron, and fresh herbs.

shopping/to-do list

1 cup celery, sliced

1 cup carrots, sliced thin

1 shallot, sliced thin

1 T garlic, minced

1 lb. fish of choice: any mix, cut into bite-size pieces

4 oz. shrimp and 2 oz. crawfish, peeled and deveined

2 saffron threads

2–3 cups fish or veggie stock

salt & pepper to taste

1 T dill, chopped

1   Cut ingredients into desired sizes.

2   Add a little oil or cooking spray of your choice to the pan. Heat pan to 375° F/medium-high heat.

3   Add carrots, celery, shallots, and garlic. Stir around for 3 minutes.

4   Add fish, shrimp, crawfish, stock, and saffron. Stir around for 4 minutes.

5   Add salt and pepper to taste. Stir around for additional minute.

Asian Fish Stir-Fry

Serves 2 Dinners/3 Lunches

`0:08` PREP `0:05` COOK

Coconut milk and hot sauce infuse the texture of fish very well. For this recipe, you can choose any type of fish: red snapper, tilapia, cod, etc., or a mix of different fish types.

shopping/to-do list

1 lb. fish filet, cut in bite-size pieces
1 T vegetable oil
1 T of each ginger, garlic, and scallion
1 cup carrot, julienne
1 cup edamame
1 T lemon grass, minced
¼ cup coconut milk
2 T soy sauce
1 T coriander
1 t sambal or Thai hot sauce
Serve over rice of choice.

1   Cut ingredients into desired sizes.

2   Add a little oil or cooking spray of your choice to the pan. Heat pan to 375° F/medium-high heat.

3   Add ginger, garlic, scallions, and carrots. Stir around for 1 minute.

4   Add fish, edamame, and lemongrass. Stir around for 2 minutes.

5   Add coconut milk, soy sauce, coriander, and sambal or hot sauce to taste. Stir around for an additional minute. Serve over rice of choice.

Sake Salmon & Crab Stir-Fry

shopping/to-do list

8–10 oz. salmon filet, cut into bite-size pieces
4 oz. crab meat chunks
1 cup scallions, sliced on the bias
1 cucumber, sliced
1 small zucchini, sliced
1 T toasted sesame seeds
Soy sauce & pepper to taste
¼ cup sake
Serve with rice noodles.

Marinade for salmon:

1 cup sake
1 T each garlic, ginger, chopped
1 t pepper

Serves 2 Dinners/3 Lunches

PREP   **COOK**

Mirin is a cooking liquid made from "mochigome" (sweet rice) and "komekoji" (yeast). It is also the traditional, ceremonial drink at New Year. Mirin adds sweetness to your marinades and dishes.

1   Cut ingredients into desired sizes. Prepare marinade and add fish for ± ½ hour.

2   Add a little oil or cooking spray of your choice to the pan. Heat pan to 375° F/medium-high heat.

3   Add salmon. Stir around for 2 minutes.

4   Add crab meat, scallions, cucumber, and zucchini. Stir around for 2 minutes.

5   Add sesame seeds and season with a little pepper and low sodium soy sauce to taste. Stir around for additional minute. Serve with rice noodles.

Szechwan Fish Stir-Fry

PREP   COOK

Szechwan pepper is not really a pepper-corn, but the berry of the Szechwan tree. It adds a spicy, peppery flavor to your dishes.

shopping/to-do list

8–10 oz. white fish, cut into bite size pieces

1 cup leek, sliced

¼ cup chives, chopped

½ cup bamboo shoots

1 T Szechwan pepper

3 T fish sauce

1 T garlic, minced

1 T fresh grated ginger

1 T low sodium soy sauce

Serve over rice or egg noodles.

1. Cut ingredients into desired sizes.

2. Add a little oil or cooking spray of your choice to the pan. Heat pan to 375° F/medium-high heat.

3. Add fish. Stir around for 2 minutes.

4. Add leek, chives, bamboo shoots, fish sauce, garlic, and ginger. Stir around for 2 minutes.

5. Add Szechwan pepper and low sodium soy sauce to taste. Stir around for an additional minute. Serve over rice or egg noodles.

Caribbean Fish Stir-Fry

Serves 2 Dinners/3 Lunches

PREP 0:10   **COOK** 0:05

In the Caribbean, these fish are being caught fresh daily in abundance: catfish, cod, conch, crab, grouper, lobster, shrimp, snapper, spearfish, swordfish, and wahoo.

shopping/to-do list

8 oz. white fish filet, cut in cubes
6 oz. shrimp, peeled and deveined
1 garlic clove, minced
1 mango, peeled, small diced
1 grapefruit, cut into segments
¼ cup cream of coconut
squeeze of lime juice
¼ cup Caribbean rum (optional)
½ cup cilantro leaves
hot sauce, salt & pepper to taste
Serve over rice of choice.

1 Cut ingredients into desired sizes.

2 Add a little oil or cooking spray of your choice to the pan. Heat pan to 375° F/medium-high heat.

3 Add fish and shrimp. Stir around for 2 minutes.

4 Add garlic, mango, grapefruit, and cream of coconut. Stir around for 1 minute.

5 Add lime juice, rum, cilantro, and season with salt, pepper, and hot sauce to taste. Stir around for an additional minute. Serve over rice of choice.

Sea Bass Farfalle Stir-Fry

shopping/to-do list

8 oz. sea bass, cut into bite-size pieces
1 cup portobello mushroom, sliced
2 tomatoes, diced
1 T capers
1/3 cup tarragon leaves
1/4 cup limoncello (or lemon juice)
salt & pepper to taste
Serve with cooked farfalle
(bow tie) pasta.

0:08 PREP

0:06 COOK

Farfalle is a bow-tie shaped pasta, available in different flavors: basil, black pepper, garlic, parsley, red pimento, saffron, spinach, and tri-color. Striped farfalle is a flavor combination of egg, spinach, and tomato.

1 Cut ingredients into the desired sizes.

2 Add a little oil or cooking spray of your choice to the pan. Heat pan to 375° F/medium-high heat.

3 Add sea bass. Stir around for 2 minutes to brown on all sides.

4 Add portobello mushroom, tomatoes, and capers. Stir around for 2 minutes.

5 Add tarragon, limoncello, salt, and pepper to taste. Stir around for an additional minute. Serve with cooked farfalle pasta.

Mahi-Mahi Stir-Fry

Serves 2 Dinners/3 Lunches

`0:08` PREP   `0:06` COOK

Mahi-mahi is also known as dolphin fish (the fish, not the mammal), or dorado. It is thin-skinned with firm, light pink flesh. Mahi-mahi has a delicate flavor that is almost sweet, ideal for a variety of preparations. Stir-fry lightly; just till it flakes.

shopping/to-do list

8–10 oz. mahi-mahi, cut into thin slices
1 grapefruit, in segments
2 tomatoes, diced
1 T garlic, minced
1 t cumin
¼ cup pomegranate juice
1 T cilantro, chopped
salt & pepper to taste
Serve over rice or sweet potatoes.

1   Cut ingredients into desired sizes.

2   Add a little oil or cooking spray of your choice to the pan. Heat pan to 375° F/medium-high heat.

3   Add mahi-mahi. Stir around for 2 minutes.

4   Add grapefruit, tomato, garlic, and cumin. Stir around for 2 minutes.

5   Add pomegranate juice, cilantro, and season with sea salt and pepper to taste. Stir around for an additional minute. Serve over rice or sweet potatoes.

Hawaiian Swordfish Stir-Fry

Serves 2 Dinners/3 Lunches

`0:10` PREP   `0:05` COOK

Swordfish, also known as broadbill swordfish, or "shutome" in Hawaii, tends to have a higher oil content, a richer flavor and a texture similar to that of premium cuts of beef.

1   Cut ingredients into desired sizes.

2   Add a little oil or cooking spray of your choice to the pan. Heat pan to 375° F/ medium-high heat.

3   Add swordfish. Stir around for 2 minutes.

4   Add pineapple, tomato, and ginger. Stir around for 2 minutes.

5   Add rosemary, coconut, pepper, and low sodium soy sauce to taste. Stir around for an additional minute. Serve with noodles or rice, and garnish with seaweed strips.

Fish & Escarole Stir-Fry

Serves 2 Dinners/3 Lunches

```
0:07        0:05
PREP        COOK
```

A traditional "Friday comfort food" in many European households. The flaky fish texture infuses well with the fresh minced garlic and escarole leaves, which wilt slightly due to the heat but keep their iron and vitamins due to the short wok time.

1   Cut ingredients into desired sizes.

2   Add a little oil or cooking spray of your choice to the pan. Heat pan to 375° F/ medium-high heat.

3   Add fish. Stir around for 2 minutes.

4   Add escarole, garlic, and lemon juice. Stir around for 1 minute.

5   Add wine and pine nuts and season with sea salt and white pepper to taste. Stir around for an additional minute. Serve over rice or mashed potatoes.

Scandinavian Salmon Stir-Fry

shopping/to-do list

8–10 oz. salmon filet, bite-size pieces
¼ cup lemon concassee or 2 T juice
2 T capers
2 leeks, white part sliced,
washed and drained
1 t coarse black pepper
¼ cup aquavit (or fish stock)
Serve with roasted potatoes and garnish with
dill.

Serves 2 Dinners/3 Lunches

0:15
PREP

0:06
COOK

Scandinavia is the group of countries: Denmark, Norway, Finland, and Sweden. Although they each have their own cultures and cuisines, they also have a lot in common, like their love of fresh salmon and aquavit.

1   Cut ingredients into desired sizes.

2   Add a little oil or cooking spray of your choice to the pan. Heat pan to 375° F/medium-high heat.

3   Add salmon. Stir around for 2 minutes.

4   Add lemon concassee, capers, and leek. Stir around for 2 minutes.

5   Add black pepper and aquavit. Stir around for an additional minute. Serve with roasted potatoes and garnish with dill.

Tropical Sea Bass Stir-Fry

Serves 2 Dinners/3 Lunches

0:08 PREP   **0:06** COOK

shopping/to-do list

8–10 oz. sea bass, cut into bite-size pieces
1 cup green bell pepper, sliced thin
½ cup coconut milk
1 cup watermelon, cubed small
squeeze of lime juice
1 T fresh grated ginger
salt & pepper to taste
1 T cilantro, chopped
1 t lime zest
Serve on a bed of Forbidden Rice(see page 30).

In Hawaii, its name is Hapu'upu'u. As a member of the grouper family, the sea bass is able to change skin colors to blend into its natural habitat. It is noted for its clear white flesh and delicate flavor. Great for stir-fries, sweet-and-sour fish recipes, and fish-head soup.

1 Cut ingredients into desired sizes.

2 Add a little oil or cooking spray of your choice to the pan. Heat pan to 375° F/ medium-high heat.

3 Add sea bass. Stir around for 2 minutes.

4 Add bell pepper, coconut milk, watermelon, lime juice, and ginger. Add salt and pepper to taste. Stir around for 2 minutes.

5 Serve over "Forbidden Rice"* (see rice info on page 30), and garnish with chopped cilantro and lime zest.

Simply Fish Stir-Fry

Serves 2 Dinners/3 Lunches

`0:11`
PREP

`0:06`
COOK

Oily fish, like anchovies, herring, mackerel, tuna, salmon, and sardines are great health sources to help lower bad cholesterol levels and increase good cholesterol levels.

shopping/to do list

8 oz. red snapper filet, cut into
bite-size pieces
6 oz. white fish filet (cod, whiting, flounder,
etc.) cut into bite-size pieces
2 cups mixed bell peppers, chopped
2 shallots, chopped
1 t lemon juice
1 T fish sauce
salt & pepper to taste
Serve over rice or noodles.

1. Cut ingredients into desired sizes.

2. Add a little oil or cooking spray of your choice to the pan. Heat pan to 375° F/medium-high heat.

3. Add fish. Stir around for 2 minutes.

4. Add mixed bell peppers, shallots, lemon juice, and fish sauce. Stir around for 2 minutes.

5. Add salt and pepper to taste. Stir around for an additional minute. Serve over rice of choice, like Bhutanese red rice (see page 30 for more rice info).

Sweet & Sour Flounder Stir-Fry

shopping/to-do list

1 cup sugar snap peas
1 T scallion, sliced on the bias
1 t lemon grass, minced finely
8–12 oz. flounder filet, bite-size pieces
2 T cream or half & half
squeeze of kaffir lime juice
sea salt & pepper to taste
Serve over rice or noodles.

Serves 2 Dinners/3 Lunches

0:08 PREP   0:05 COOK

This flatfish is cut into filets, and in the Southeast sold with some skin on. The flesh is easy to digest. Delicious braised, broiled, fried, steamed, and stir-fried.

1   Cut ingredients into desired sizes.

2   Add a little oil or cooking spray of your choice to the pan. Heat pan to 375° F/medium-high heat.

3   Add sugar snap peas, scallions, and lemongrass. Stir around for 1 minute.

4   Add flounder. Stir around for 2 minutes.

5   Add cream lime juice and season with sea salt and white pepper to taste. Stir around for additional minute. Serve over rice or noodles.

Japanese Tuna Stir-Fry

Serves 2 Dinners/3 Lunches

0:05 PREP   **0:04 COOK**

Bigeye tuna is one of two species known in Hawaii as ahi. Bigeye tuna typically has a higher fat content than yellowfin and is preferred over yellowfin by more discriminating sashimi eaters. It is also great for stir-fries due to a short wok time.

shopping/to-do list

1 cup shiitake mushrooms, sliced
1 T garlic, minced
1 T ginger, freshly grated
1 T scallion, cut on the bias
8–10 oz. tuna, sliced thin
1 T toasted sesame seeds
2 T low sodium soy sauce
2 T mirin
1 t wasabi powder
black pepper
Serve over rice of choice.

1   Cut ingredients into desired sizes.

2   Add a little oil or cooking spray of your choice to the pan. Heat pan to 375° F/medium-high heat.

3   Add mushrooms, garlic, ginger, and scallion. Stir around for 2 minutes.

4   Add tuna, mirin, and sesame seeds. Season with pepper and low sodium soy sauce to taste. Stir around for < 1 minute for "medium rare" and 2 minutes for "well done." Serve over rice of choice.

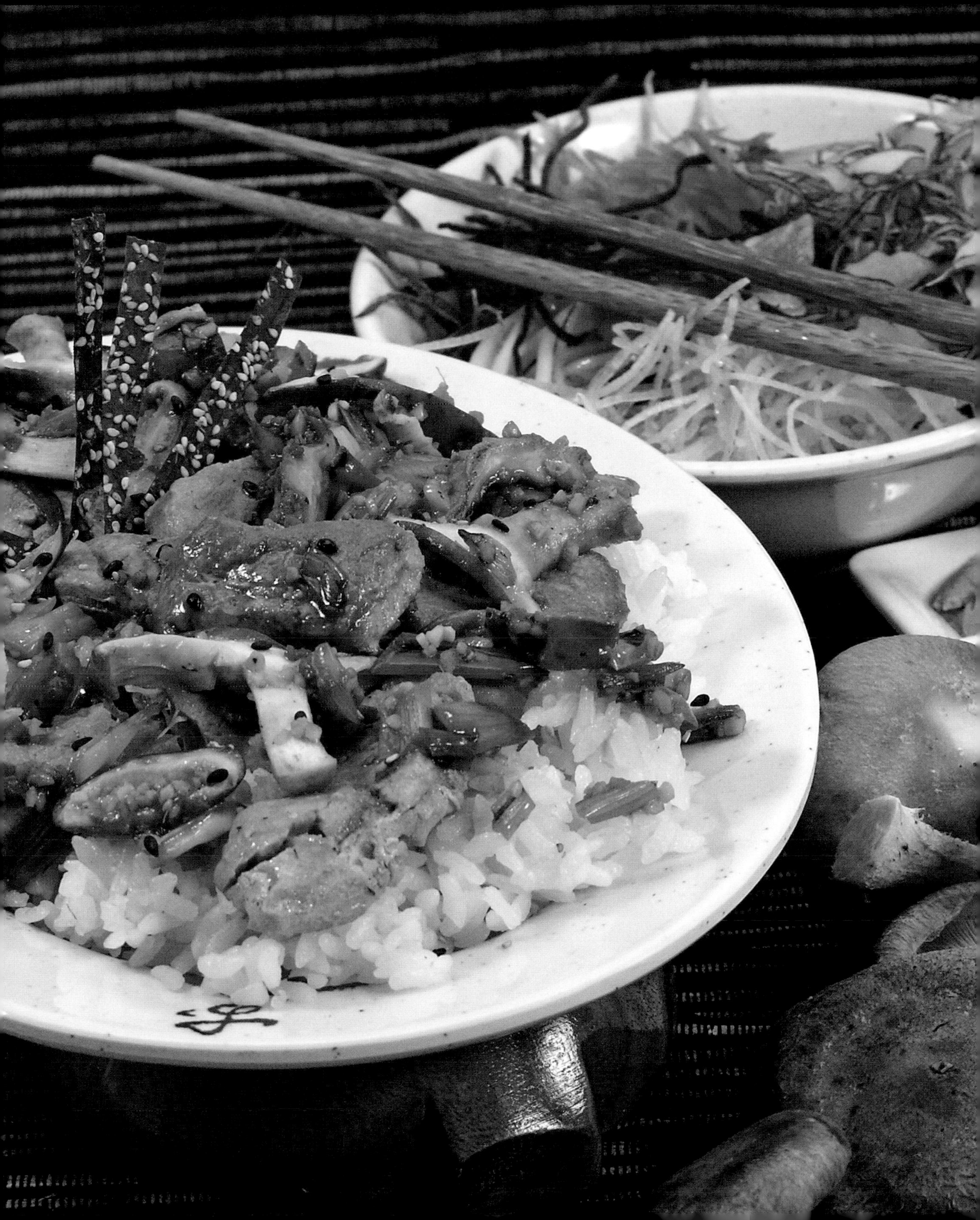

Mexican Cod Stir-Fry

Serves 2 Dinners/3 Lunches

0:10	0:05
PREP	COOK

Cod is a popular fish in Mexican cuisine used in soups, tacos, and cod cakes. The texture of cod is very suitable for a delicious stir-fry.

shopping/to-do list

8–10 oz. cod, cut into bite-size pieces

1 onion, small diced

2 tomatoes, diced

1 T Mexican blend spices

1 small jalapeño, chopped

squeeze lime juice

1 T cilantro, chopped

1 t red crushed pepper

¼ cup tequila

Serve with rice of choice.

1   Cut ingredients into desired sizes.

2   Add a little oil or cooking spray of your choice to the pan. Heat pan to 375° F/medium-high heat.

3   Add onion. Stir around for 1 minute.

4   Add cod, tomatoes, Mexican spices, jalapeño, and lime juice. Stir around for 2 minutes.

5   Add red crushed pepper, cilantro, and tequila. Stir around for an additional minute. Serve with rice of choice.

3

Lamb

A lamb is a sheep that is less than one year old. Its pale, pink meat is tender, its cooking time is short, and its flavor is mild. Lamb for stir-fry is available ground or in steaks.

Greek Lamb Stir-Fry

Serves 2 Dinners/3 Lunches

`0:05` **PREP**   `0:05` **COOK**

Greek cuisine is informal and unpretentious with bold flavors of fresh herbs, rich-flavored fruits and vegetables, and intense taste of local cheese, wine, olives, and grapes.

shopping/to-do list

8–12 oz. ground lamb, rolled into small meatballs

1 eggplant, diced small

1 tomato, diced medium

2 T Greek olive, sliced

1 t star anise, ground

½ t ground cloves

1 T marjoram

1 T garlic, minced

2 T olive oil

salt & pepper to taste

Serve with warm grape wraps and garlic yogurt sauce (page 230).

1 Cut all ingredients into described sizes.

2 Add a little oil or cooking spray of your choice to the pan. Heat pan to 400°F/high heat.

3 Add lamb. Stir around for 2 minutes to brown on all sides.

4 Add eggplant, tomato, olives, and marjoram. Stir around for 1 minute.

5 Add star anise, ground clove, salt, and pepper to taste. Stir around for an additional minute. Serve with warm grape wraps and garlic yogurt sauce (page 230).

Curried Lamb Stir-Fry

Serves 2 Dinners/3 Lunches

0:07 PREP   **0:06** COOK

The cuisine of India uses many spices chosen for their medicinal benefits. Cloves, cardamom, turmeric, and garlic are just a few examples of extraordinary spices with powerful health benefits.

shopping/to-do list

8–12 oz. lamb, cut into bite-size pieces
2 shallots, minced
1 cup cabbage, sliced
2 T cilantro leaves

Wet Rub:

2 T coconut milk
½ T curry or turmeric powder
1 t caraway
1 t cayenne pepper
salt & pepper to taste
Serve over rice of choice and
garnish with cilantro sprigs.

1   Cut all ingredients into described sizes. Mix the wet-rub ingredients and rub them on the meat.

2   Add a little oil or cooking spray of your choice to the pan. Heat pan to 400°F/high heat.

3   Add lamb. Stir around for 2 minutes to brown on all sides.

4   Add shallots and cabbage. Stir around for 2 minutes.

5   Add cilantro, and little salt and pepper to taste. Stir around for an additional minute. Serve over rice of choice, and garnish with a few cilantro sprigs.

North African Lamb Stir-Fry

Serves 2 Dinners/3 Lunches

0:08 PREP   **0:06** COOK

Magreb is the cuisine from North Africa, Morocco, and Algeria, loaded with bold and sweet flavors, combined with cinnamon, cloves and coriander.

shopping/to-do list

8–12 oz. lamb, cut into bite-size pieces
1 cup carrots, shredded
½ cup raisins, soaked and drained
¼ cup pecans, chopped
1 t cinnamon
1 t cloves, ground
1 t honey
⅓ cup pomegranate juice
Serve with couscous and garlic yogurt sauce
(see page 230).

1   Cut all ingredients into described sizes.

2   Add a little oil or cooking spray of your choice to the pan. Heat pan to 400°F/high heat.

3   Add lamb. Stir around for 2 minutes to brown on all sides.

4   Add carrot. Add raisins, pecans, cinnamon, cloves, honey, and pomegranate juice. Stir around for 2 minutes.

5   Serve over couscous and garlic yogurt sauce (see page 230).

Indonesian Lamb Stir-Fry

Serves 2 Dinners/3 Lunches

`0:15` PREP   `0:06` COOK

Bali is one of the beautiful islands of Indonesia, and Kambing Mekuah is a traditional Balinese lamb dish that is part of their rich, flavorful, and exotic cuisine.

shopping/to do list

8–12 oz. lamb, cut into bite-size pieces
½ cup leek, sliced
½ cup coy bean sprouts
1 small onion, sliced thin
1 green hot pepper, chopped
1 t lemon grass, chopped
1 T garlic, minced
1 t cardamom seeds, fresh ground
⅓ cup coconut milk
½ T cayenne pepper
1 T low sodium soy sauce
Serve over rice or noodles of choice.

1   Cut all ingredients into described sizes.

2   Add a little oil or cooking spray of your choice to the pan. Heat pan to 400°F/high heat.

3   Add lamb. Stir around for 2 minutes to brown on all sides.

4   Add leek, bean sprouts, onion, hot pepper, lemongrass, garlic, and cardamom. Stir around for 2 minutes.

5   Add coconut milk, cayenne pepper, and low sodium soy sauce to taste. Stir around for an additional minute. Serve over rice or noodles of choice.

Mediterranean Lamb Stir-Fry

Serves 2 Dinners/3 Lunches

0:08	0:06
PREP	COOK

shopping/to-do list

8–12 oz. lamb, cut into bite-size pieces
1 cup zucchini, cut into half moons
1 cup mushrooms, sliced
1 cup artichoke hearts, diced
1 T garlic, minced
2 T pine nuts
1 cup grapes, cut in half
sea salt & black pepper to taste
2 T fresh mint leaves
Serve over rice, pasta, or couscous.

In Mediterranean cuisine, lamb is often used in stews and as a ground meat. For our stir-fry version, we use steak cut into bite-size pieces. Small meatballs are also great to use.

1   Cut all ingredients into described sizes.

2   Add a little oil or cooking spray of your choice to the pan. Heat pan to 400°F/high heat.

3   Add lamb. Stir around for 2 minutes to brown on all sides.

4   Add zucchini, mushrooms, artichoke hearts, garlic, pine nuts, and grapes. Stir around for 2 minutes.

5   Add a little salt and pepper to taste. Stir around for an additional minute. Serve over rice, pasta, or couscous, and garnish with mint leaves.

New Zealand Stir-Fry

0:15 PREP   0:06 COOK

The New Zealand lamb is a source of the finest quality wool. Its tender meat is known for its succulent flavor.

shopping/to-do list

8–12 oz. lamb, cut into bite-size pieces
1 cup white beans, cooked/canned
1 small onion, sliced thin
1 green hot pepper, chopped
1 T garlic, minced
1 cup kiwi, peeled, sliced into half moons
1 T fresh grated ginger
½ T white pepper
1 T low sodium soy sauce

1 Cut all ingredients into described sizes.

2 Add a little oil or cooking spray of your choice to the pan. Heat pan to 400°F/high heat.

3 Add lamb. Stir around for 2 minutes to brown on all sides.

4 Add beans, onion, hot pepper, garlic, and ginger. Stir around for 2 minutes.

5 Add kiwi and season with pepper and low sodium soy sauce to taste. Stir around for an additional minute.

_4_

Pork

Choose lean pork and cut away fat.
Try pork tenderloin, boneless pork
chops, pre-cut, or stir-fry pork.

Hawaiian Pork Stir-Fry

Serves 2 Dinners/3 Lunches

PREP 0:10   COOK 0:06

The pineapple is one of the tropical fruits grown on the islands of Hawaii. Jim Dole founded the company in 1851, and today, Dole Food Company has a great website with educational and nutritional information. Check out www.dole.com.

1   Cut ingredients into desired sizes.

2   Add a little oil or cooking spray of your choice to the pan. Heat pan to 400°F/high heat.

3   Add pork and onion. Stir around for 2 minutes to brown on all sides.

4   Add bell pepper and pineapple. Stir around for 2 minutes.

5   Add nuts and seasoning to taste. Stir around for an additional 1 minute. Serve over cooked rice of choice.

Basque Ham Stir-Fry

Serves 2 Dinners/3 Lunches

PREP   COOK

Basque Country is the northern province in Spain. The traditional Basque dish is transformed into this stir-fry recipe that will satisfy your appetite.

shopping/to-do list

6–8 oz. Bayonne ham, sliced ¼" thick, cubed
2 peppers, cut into paysanne-size pieces (see Intro.)
3 tomotoes, diced small
I cup wild mushrooms, sliced
black pepper, fresh ground
± ½ T paprika
sea salt to taste
Serve over yellow rice.

1   Cut ingredients into desired sizes.

2   Add a little oil or cooking spray of your choice to the pan. Heat pan to 400°F/high heat.

3   Add ham and peppers. Stir around for 2 minutes.

4   Add tomatoes and mushrooms. Stir around for 2 minutes.

5   Add sea salt, pepper, and paprika powder to taste. Stir around for an additional minute. Serve over yellow rice.

Mexican Pork Stir-Fry

Serves 2 Dinners/3 Lunches

PREP   COOK

Mexican ingredients are not limited to tomatoes, cumin, and corn. The cuisine is simple, but the flavors are rich, intense, and bold.

shopping/to-do list

8–12 oz. lean pork, cut into ½" strips
1 bell pepper, chopped
1 T jalapeño, sliced
4 scallions, sliced
1 tomato, diced small
2 tomatillos, diced small
½ cup corn kernels
1 t garlic, minced
1 t cumin
1 t coriander
2 T cilantro leaves
Served in warm tortilla wraps.

1   Cut ingredients into desired sizes.

2   Add a little oil or cooking spray of your choice to the pan. Heat pan to 400°F/high heat.

3   Add pork. Stir around for 2 minutes to brown on all sides.

4   Add bell pepper, jalapeño, scallions, tomato, tomatillo, corn, and garlic. Stir around for 2 minutes.

5   Add cumin, coriander, cilantro leaves, salt, and pepper to taste. Stir around for an additional minute. Served in warm tortilla wraps.

Colorful Pork Stir-Fry

Serves 2 Dinners/3 Lunches

PREP   COOK

shopping/to-do list

8–12 oz. lean pork, cut into bite-size pieces
⅓ red bell pepper, sliced thin
⅓ green bell pepper, sliced thin
⅓ yellow bell pepper, sliced thin
⅓ orange bell pepper, sliced thin
2 T black olives, sliced
1 T garlic, minced
1 T sage, chopped
¼ cup red wine (optional)
salt & pepper to taste
Serve over rice or pasta.

This recipe is the base for many infusions. The pork, onion, and bell peppers are the main ingredients, but the seasoning will define the cuisine. Be creative and try different spice and herb combinations. (See flavor intro pages.)

1   Cut ingredients into desired sizes.

2   Add a little oil or cooking spray of your choice to the pan. Heat pan to 400°F/high heat.

3   Add pork. Stir around for 2 minutes to brown on all sides.

4   Add bell pepper slices, black olives, and garlic. Stir around for 2 minutes.

5   Add sage, wine, salt, and pepper to taste. Stir around for 2 minutes. Serve over cooked rice or pasta. Garnish with sage leaves.

Ham & Lentil Stir-Fry

Serves 2 Dinners/3 Lunches

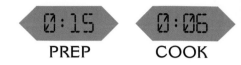

PREP   COOK

Lentils are small, soft-textured beans, and are available in red, yellow, and green. They are used in a wide variety of cuisines from all over the world and are a great source of vitamins, fiber, and calcium.

1   Cut ingredients into desired sizes.

2   Add a little oil or cooking spray of your choice to the pan. Heat pan to 400°F/high heat.

3   Add carrot, beans, and cooked lentils. Stir around for 2 minutes.

4   Add ham and chestnuts. Season with salt and pepper. Stir around for additional 2 minutes. Serve with mashed, sweet potatoes.

Pork & Cactus Pear Stir-Fry

Serves 2 Dinners/3 Lunches

PREP   COOK

shopping/to-do list

8–12 oz. lean pork, cut into ½" strips
3 cactus pears, cut in half, scooped out,
and chopped
3 Belgium endives, ¼" slices
salt & pepper to taste
Serve over rice or mashed potatoes.

Cactus pear is also called the prickly pear cactus, and it grows in many parts of the world. The egg-shaped berry has a melon-like flavor.

1   Cut ingredients into desired sizes.

2   Add a little oil or cooking spray of your choice to the pan. Heat pan to 400°F/high heat.

3   Add pork. Stir around for 2 minutes to brown on all sides.

4   Add cactus pear and Belgium endive. Stir around for 2 minutes.

5   Add a little salt and pepper to taste. Stir around for an additional minute. Serve over rice or mashed potatoes.

Vietnamese Pork Stir-Fry

Serves 2 Dinners/3 Lunches

PREP   COOK

shopping/to-do list

8–12 oz. lean pork, bite-size pieces
2 cups cabbage, sliced
1 hot pepper, finely chopped
1 T garlic, minced
2 T basil, chopped
1 T lemongrass, finely chopped
2 T low sodium soy sauce
1 T fish sauce
black pepper, fresh ground
Served with rice or noodles

Preparing food is an art in Vietnamese cuisine with influences of French cuisine and Confucianism, which included inventions like the wok and chopsticks.

1   Cut ingredients into desired sizes.

2   Add a little oil or cooking spray of your choice to the pan. Heat pan to 400°F/high heat.

3   Add pork. Stir around for 2 minutes to brown on all sides.

4   Add cabbage, hot pepper, and garlic. Stir around for 2 minutes.

5   Add basil, lemongrass, and season with a little pepper, fish sauce, and low sodium soy sauce to taste. Stir around for an additional minute. Serve with rice or noodles of choice.

Korean Pork & Daikon Stir-Fry

Serves 2 Dinners/3 Lunches

PREP   COOK

Korean food tends to be spicier than Chinese or Japanese cuisine. This hotness comes from small chiles known as Thai chiles (heat-index 9).

shopping/to-do list

8–12 oz. lean pork, cut into ½" strips
1 Korean daikon, peeled and cubed
1 shallot, sliced thin
4 small hot peppers, chopped
1 T fresh grated ginger
2 T sesame seeds, toasted
pinch of brown sugar
1 T white pepper
1 T low sodium soy sauce
Serve with rice of choice.

1 Cut ingredients into desired sizes.

2 Add a little oil or cooking spray of your choice to the pan. Heat pan to 400°F/high heat.

3 Add pork. Stir around for 2 minutes to brown on all sides.

4 Add daikon, shallots, hot peppers, and ginger. Stir around for 2 minutes.

5 Add sesame seeds, pinch of sugar, white pepper, and low sodium soy sauce to taste. Stir around for an additional minute. Serve with rice of choice.

Italian Pork Stir-Fry

PREP 0:07 **COOK** 0:06

shopping/to-do list

8-12 oz. lean pork, cut into ½" strips
1 medium onion, sliced
3 oz. prosciutto ham, cut into ½" strips
1 T olive oil
2 sweet peppers, cut into small pieces
⅓ cup black olives, sliced
2 cups tomatoes, diced
1 T garlic, minced
sea salt & black pepper
fresh basil or oregano
Serve over pasta of choice.

Italian recipes differ from city to city, from province to province, and from family to family. The first Roman cookbook was written more than 2,000 years ago, but many recipes go from mother to daughter without being written down at all.

1. Cut ingredients into desired sizes.

2. Add a little oil or cooking spray of your choice to the pan. Heat pan to 400°F/high heat.

3. Add pork and onion. Stir around for 2 minutes.

4. Add sweet pepper, olives, tomato, ham, and garlic. Stir around for 2 minutes.

5. Add sea salt and black pepper to taste. Stir around for an additional minute. Serve over pasta of choice and garnish with fresh basil or oregano.

Pork & Shrimp Chow Mein Stir-Fry

shopping/to-do list

8–12 oz lean pork, cut into ½" strips
4 oz. shrimp, peeled and deveined
1 cup choy of choice, sliced
½ cup mushrooms of choice, sliced
½ cup Chinese cabbage, sliced
2 T bamboo shoots
1 T soy sauce
1 t Chinese 5-spice
1½ cups cooked chow mein noodles

Serves 2 Dinners/3 Lunches

PREP   COOK

Chow mein is Cantonese for fried egg noodles, which come in a wide variety. Some have to be cooked, some can just be soaked in hot water for 2 minutes. For more noodle information see pages 28–29.

1. Cut ingredients into desired sizes.

2. Add a little oil or cooking spray of your choice to the pan. Heat pan to 400°F/high heat.

3. Add pork. Stir around for 2 minutes to brown on all sides.

4. Add shrimp, stir for 1 minute. Then add choy of choice, mushrooms, Chinese cabbage, and bamboo shoots. Stir around for 2 minutes.

5. Add Chinese 5-spice, and low sodium soy sauce to taste. Add chow mein noodles. Stir around for an additional minute. Serve immediately. Look at your grocery store for some authentic "fortune cookies."

Indonesian Pork Stir-Fry

Serves 2 Dinners/3 Lunches

PREP   COOK

Rice is the main staple in most Indonesian recipes. Sambal is a fiery hot sauce that comes in a variety of different heat-indexes to spice up fish, meat, poultry, and vegetable dishes.

shopping/to-do list

8–12 oz. lean pork, cut into ½" strips
1 cup dried plums, soaked in water,
drained, sliced
1 cup carrots, shredded
2 small hot peppers, finely chopped
1 t cumin
½ t cinnamon
1 T fresh chopped coriander
salt & pepper to taste
Serve over rice of choice.

1   Cut ingredients into desired sizes.

2   Add a little oil or cooking spray of your choice to the pan. Heat pan to 400°F/high heat.

3   Add pork. Stir around for 2 minutes to brown on all sides.

4   Add drained plums, carrot, hot pepper, cumin, cinnamon, and coriander. Stir around for 2 minutes.

5   Add a little salt and pepper to taste. Stir around for an additional minute. Serve over rice of choice.

Fruity Pork Stir-Fry

Serves 2 Dinners/3 Lunches

0:07
PREP

0:06
COOK

Dried fruits are delicious ingredients that infuse well with all types of meat. The sweetness of the fruit gives an extra dimension to the savory flavor of the meat.

shopping/to-do list

8–12 oz. lean pork, cut into
bite-size pieces
1 cup of dried fruit: apricots,
plums, raisins, cranberries,
soaked and drained
1 medium onion, sliced
1 sweet pepper, cut into small pieces
1 T garlic, minced
½ cup white wine or stock
sea salt & black pepper
Serve over rice or pasta of choice.

1   Cut ingredients into desired sizes.

2   Add a little oil or cooking spray of your choice to the pan. Heat pan to 400°F/high heat.

3   Add pork. Stir around for 2 minutes.

4   Add fruit, onion, sweet pepper, and garlic. Stir around for 2 minutes.

5   Add wine or stock, sea salt, and black pepper to taste. Stir around for an additional minute. Serve over pasta of choice.

5

Poultry

Poultry is more than just a chicken breast. You can choose chicken tenderloins, boneless thighs, turkey tenderloins, boneless turkey thighs, or duck breasts.

Asian Turkey Meatball Stir-Fry

shopping/to-do list

8–10 oz. ground turkey, small meatballs
1 red bell pepper, diced medium
½ bag (4 oz.) carrots, julienned
1 zucchini, sliced thin
1 cup soybean sprouts
1 T each garlic, ginger, scallions, chopped
⅓ cup low sodium soy sauce
2 T mirin
1 cup rice or noodles of choice, cooked

Serves 2 Dinners/3 Lunches

0:10 PREP   **0:07** COOK

Making meatballs is now easier than ever. In less than a minute, you make 9 identically shaped meatballs that will cook evenly. You can choose ground turkey or chicken for this recipe. See page 241 for Meatball Magic.

1 Wash veggies, and cut them into described sizes.

2 Add a little oil or cooking spray of your choice to the pan. Heat pan to 400°F/high heat.

3 Add meatballs. Stir around for 2 minutes until all sides are brown.

4 Add bell pepper, julienned carrot, and zucchini slices. Stir around for 2 minutes.

5 Add soybean sprouts, garlic, ginger, scallions, low sodium soy sauce, and mirin to taste. Stir around for 2 minutes. Serve over cooked rice or noodles of choice.

Chicken & Ratatouille Stir-Fry

shopping/to-do list

8–10 oz. chicken breast, cut into
bite-size pieces
1 eggplant, small cubed
½ yellow and ½ green squash, sliced into half
moons
1 onion, sliced thin
2½ bell peppers in color of choice, sliced thin
2 tomatoes, diced small
1 T garlic
1 T Tomato paste
herbs: basil, oregano, thyme to taste
Serve over rice or mashed potatoes.

Serves 2 Dinners/3 Lunches

PREP   COOK

Ratatouille is a traditional French side dish, especially popular in Provence where fresh eggplant, squash, and herbs grow in abundance.

1   Cut ingredients into desired sizes.

2   Add a little oil or cooking spray of your choice to the pan. Heat pan to 400°F/high heat.

3   Add chicken. Stir around for 2 minutes to brown on all sides.

4   Add eggplant, squash, onion, bell pepper, tomato, garlic, and tomato paste. Stir around for 2 minutes.

5   Add herbs of choice, sea salt, and pepper to taste. Stir around for an additional minute. Serve over rice or mashed potatoes.

Vietnamese Chicken Stir-Fry

shopping/to-do list

8–10 oz. chicken breast, cut into
½" strips
1½ cup sugar snap peas
1½ cup mushrooms, sliced
1 T lemongrass, minced
1 shallot, sliced thin
1 red hot pepper, chopped
1 T garlic, minced
1 T fresh grated ginger
1 T white pepper
1 T low sodium soy sauce
Serve over rice or noodles of choice.

Serves 2 Dinners/3 Lunches

PREP 0:15   COOK 0:06

Vietnamese cuisine is infused with French culinary characteristics due to the occupation of Vietnam by the French. The infusion of the two cuisines is a very interesting culinary journey.

1. Cut ingredients into desired sizes.

2. Add a little oil or cooking spray of your choice to the pan. Heat pan to 400°F/high heat.

3. Add chicken. Stir around for 2 minutes to brown on all sides.

4. Add peas, mushrooms, lemongrass, shallots, hot pepper, garlic, and ginger. Stir around for 2 minutes.

5. Add pepper and low sodium soy sauce to taste. Stir around for an additional minute. Serve over rice or noodles of choice.

Chicken Liver Stir-Fry

shopping/to-do list

8–10 oz. chicken livers, cut into
½" strips
1 small onion, sliced thin
1 Anaheim pepper, chopped
1 T garlic, minced
1 apple, cored and sliced
2 bananas, sliced
1 t turmeric powder
1 T Madeira
½ t sea salt
Serve over rice or mashed potatoes.

Serves 2 Dinners/3 Lunches

0:09 PREP   **0:06** COOK

Research has indicated that turmeric, the yellow spice, helps in the fight against Alzheimer's disease. One tablespoon a day is recommended. Turmeric can also be added to a glass of warm milk.

1   Cut ingredients into desired sizes.

2   Add a little oil or cooking spray of your choice to the pan. Heat pan to 400°F/high heat.

3   Add chicken. Stir around for 2 minutes to brown on all sides.

4   Add onion, pepper, garlic, apple, and banana. Stir around for 2 minutes.

5   Add turmeric, Madeira, and salt. Stir around for an additional minute. Serve over rice or mashed potatoes

Festive Turkey Stir-Fry

Serves 2 Dinners/3 Lunches

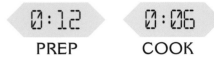

0:12 PREP   0:06 COOK

Not in the mood for a lot of leftover turkey meat? Just buy ground turkey (for meatballs) or a nice piece of turkey tenderloin and prepare this easy stir-fry dish that has all the flavor, color, and feel of the holidays.

1   Cut ingredients into desired sizes.

2   Add a little oil or cooking spray of your choice to the pan. Heat pan to 400°F/high heat.

3   Add turkey. Stir around for 2 minutes to brown on all sides.

4   Add celery, bell pepper, garlic, ginger, and cranberry sauce. Stir around for 2 minutes.

5   Add red crushed pepper and low sodium soy sauce to taste. Stir around for an additional minute. Serve over mashed or pearl potatoes.

Chicken & Bean Sprout Stir-Fry

shopping/to-do list

8–10 oz. chicken breast, cut into ½" strips
1 cup bok choy, sliced
1½ cup soybean sprouts
½ cup celery, sliced
1 small onion, sliced
1 green hot pepper, chopped
1 T garlic, minced
1 T fresh grated ginger
1 T Szechwan pepper
1 T low sodium soy sauce
1 cup rice noodles

Serves 2 Dinners/3 Lunches

0:10 PREP   **0:05** COOK

Sprouts are high in vitamin A and come in many shapes, sizes, colors, and flavors. This Chicken & Bean Sprout Stir-Fry is an easy dish for a lunch or dinner that everybody loves.

1 Cut ingredients into desired sizes. Soak rice noodles in hot water for 3 minutes.

2 Add a little oil or cooking spray of your choice to the pan. Heat pan to 400°F/high heat.

3 Add chicken. Stir around for 2 minutes to brown on all sides.

4 Add bok choy, bean sprouts, celery, onion, hot pepper, garlic, and ginger. Stir around for 2 minutes.

5 Add drained rice noodles, Szechwan pepper, and low sodium soy sauce to taste. Stir around for an additional minute.

Chicken & Veggie Stir-Fry

shopping/to-do list

8–10 oz. chicken breast, cut into
bite-size pieces
1 cup baby carrots
1 cup broccoli florets
1 cup snap peas
1 red (hot) pepper, chopped
1 small onion, sliced thin
1 T garlic, minced
$\frac{1}{3}$ fish sauce
1 t black pepper
1 T soy sauce
Serve over rice noodles of choice.

Serves 2 Dinners/3 Lunches

`0:15`
PREP

`0:06`
COOK

Broccoli is a family member of the cabbage family, high in vitamins A and D, and a great source of calcium. It has been a popular vegetable for more than 2,000 years in Europe and Asia. Since the 1920s, it has been available all over the world.

1   Cut ingredients into desired sizes.

2   Add a little oil or cooking spray of your choice to the pan. Heat pan to 400°F/high heat.

3   Add chicken. Stir around for 2 minutes to brown on all sides.

4   Add carrot, broccoli florets, snap peas, hot pepper, onion, and garlic. Stir around for 2 minutes.

5   Add fish sauce, pepper, and low sodium soy sauce to taste. Stir around for an additional minute. Serve over rice noodles of choice.

Caribbean Chicken Stir-Fry

shopping/to-do list

8–10 oz. chicken breast, cut into ½" strips
1 small onion, diced small
1 cup kumquats, quartered
½ orange, segmented
1 green (hot) pepper, chopped
1 T garlic, minced
½ T curry powder
1 cup mango, peeled, cubed
½ orange, juiced
sea salt & pepper to taste
Serve over rice of choice.

Serves 2 Dinners/3 Lunches

PREP   COOK

The flavor combinations of any recipe can be altered by adjusting the ingredients of your choice. For example, if you don't like hot and spicy, use a green bell pepper instead of a hot pepper.

1   Cut ingredients into desired sizes.

2   Add a little oil or cooking spray of your choice to the pan. Heat pan to 400°F/high heat.

3   Add chicken. Stir around for 2 minutes to brown on all sides.

4   Add onion, kumquats, hot pepper, garlic, and curry. Stir around for 2 minutes.

5   Add orange segments, mango, orange juice, a little sea salt, and pepper to taste. Stir around for an additional minute. Serve over rice of choice.

Chicken & Cabbage Stir-Fry

Serves 2 Dinners/3 Lunches

0:15	0:06
PREP	COOK

Ground chicken is a great substitute for ground beef, and little meatballs are easily made in seconds with the handy Meatball Magic, see page 241.

1   Cut ingredients into desired sizes.

2   Add a little oil or cooking spray of your choice to the pan. Heat pan to 400°F/high heat.

3   Add meatballs. Stir around for 2 minutes to brown on all sides.

4   Add onion, bell pepper, cabbage, and garlic. Stir around for 2 minutes.

5   Add mirin, sea salt, and pepper to taste. Stir around for an additional minute. Serve over rice of choice.

North African Chicken Stir-Fry

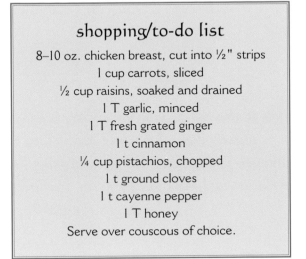

shopping/to-do list

8–10 oz. chicken breast, cut into ½" strips
1 cup carrots, sliced
½ cup raisins, soaked and drained
1 T garlic, minced
1 T fresh grated ginger
1 t cinnamon
¼ cup pistachios, chopped
1 t ground cloves
1 t cayenne pepper
1 T honey
Serve over couscous of choice.

Serves 2 Dinners/3 Lunches

0:15 PREP   **0:06** COOK

Couscous is the main staple of the North African cuisine. It is made of ground semolina, flour, and water, and is used as a main dish or combined with meat or vegetable dishes.

1   Cut ingredients into desired sizes.

2   Add a little oil or cooking spray of your choice to the pan. Heat pan to 400°F/high heat.

3   Add chicken. Stir around for 2 minutes to brown on all sides.

4   Add carrot, garlic, and ginger. Stir around for 2 minutes.

5   Add raisins, pistachios, cinnamon, ground cloves, pepper, and honey. Stir around for an additional minute. Serve over couscous.

Chicken & Escarole Stir-Fry

Serves 2 Dinners/3 Lunches

0:15 PREP   **0:06** COOK

Escarole is also called Batavian endive. It has a slightly bitter flavor and sturdy leaves; although young leaves are great in salads, a more mature and more intense flavored escarole is great in stir-fries.

1 Cut ingredients into desired sizes.

2 Add a little oil or cooking spray of your choice to the pan. Heat pan to 400°F/high heat.

3 Add chicken. Stir around for 2 minutes to brown on all sides.

4 Add onion and garlic. Stir around for 1 minute.

5 Add escarole, capers, walnuts, champagne, pepper, and salt to taste. Stir around for an additional minute. Serve over rice or potatoes of choice.

Fruity Turkey Stir-Fry

Serves 2 Dinners/3 Lunches

0:15 PREP   **0:06** COOK

Strawberries and celery go well together in salads with chicken or turkey, a little mayonnaise, salt, and pepper to taste. This stir-fry version provides an interesting infusion of flavors that will intrigue your taste buds.

1   Cut ingredients into desired sizes.

2   Add a little oil or cooking spray of your choice to the pan. Heat pan to 400°F/high heat.

3   Add chicken. Stir around for 2 minutes to brown on all sides.

4   Add celery and chestnut. Stir around for 2 minutes.

5   Add parsley, wine, strawberries, pepper, and salt to taste. Stir around for an additional minute. Serve over rice or potatoes of choice.

Sateh Atjam Stir-Fry

Serves 2 Dinners/3 Lunches

0:15 PREP   **0:06** COOK

Atjam is Indonesian for chicken, and sateh is the Indonesian indigenous sauce made of toasted peanuts, peanut oil, ketoembar (coriander), soy sauce, and sambal (Indonesian hot sauce).

1   Cut ingredients into desired sizes.

2   Add a little oil or cooking spray of your choice to the pan. Heat pan to 400°F/high heat.

3   Add chicken. Stir around for 2 minutes to brown on all sides.

4   Add carrots, celery, bean sprouts, shallot, and ginger. Stir around for 2 minutes.

5   Add ketjap and Indonesian spices to taste. Stir around for an additional minute. Serve over rice or egg noodles and top with Indonesian sateh sauce.

6

Seafood

Fresh seafood—clams, crabs, crayfish, lobster, mussels, octopus, prawns, scallops, shrimp, and squid—is great to use in stir-fries and only require a short wok time.

Shrimp Stir-Fry à la Biarritz

shopping/to-do list

1 lb. shrimp, peeled, deveined
1 bunch asparagus, cut into 1" pieces
2 shallots, finely chopped
1 T garlic, minced
sea salt & white pepper to taste
¼ cup cream or half & half
⅓ cup red wine, preferable Bordeaux
1 T dill
1 lemon concassee or 1 T zest

Serves 2 Dinners/3 Lunches

PREP   COOK

The cuisine of Biarritz has been influenced by the abundance of fresh fish and seafood, wines with great "bouquet," fresh produce, and a profusion of sunshine.

1   Cut ingredients into desired sizes.

2   Add a little oil or cooking spray of your choice to the pan. Heat pan to 375°F/medium-high heat.

3   Add shrimp. Stir around for 2 minutes.

4   Add asparagus pieces, shallot, and garlic. Stir around for 2 minutes.

5   Add cream, wine, and season with sea salt and white pepper to taste. Stir around for an additional minute. Garnish with dill and lemon concassee.

Dom Yam Gung Stir-Fry Soup

shopping/to-do list

8–12 oz. tiger shrimps, peeled and deveined
1 Thai red pepper, chopped finely
2 T lemongrass, chopped finely
2 T lime juice
2 kaffir leaves
1 T fish sauce
3 cups shrimp or veggie stock

Serves 2 Dinners/3 Lunches

PREP   COOK

Dom Yam Gung Stir-Fry Soup is a traditional and popular Thai dish that is easily and quickly prepared in the wok.

1   Cut ingredients into desired sizes.

2   Add a little oil or cooking spray of your choice to the pan. Heat pan to 375°F/medium-high heat.

3   Add shrimp. Stir around for 2 minutes. The shrimp will turn orange.

4   Add hot pepper, lemongrass, lime juice, kaffir leaves, and ginger. Stir around for 2 minutes.

5   Add stock and season to taste. Bring to a boil. Stir around for an additional minute.

Warm Crayfish Stir-Fry Salad

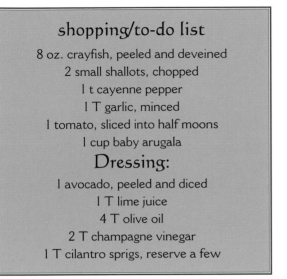

shopping/to-do list

8 oz. crayfish, peeled and deveined
2 small shallots, chopped
1 t cayenne pepper
1 T garlic, minced
1 tomato, sliced into half moons
1 cup baby arugala

Dressing:

1 avocado, peeled and diced
1 T lime juice
4 T olive oil
2 T champagne vinegar
1 T cilantro sprigs, reserve a few

Serves 2 Dinners/3 Lunches

PREP 0:12   **COOK** 0:06

Crayfish are a small version of the lobster family, ranging from 3 to 6 inches. In the south of the United States, they are called crawfish. To celebrate their arrival, festivals are held all over the south, from Louisiana to Jacksonville, FL.

1   Cut ingredients into desired sizes. Mix dressing ingredients in separate bowl.

2   Add a little oil or cooking spray of your choice to the pan. Heat pan to 375°F/medium-high heat.

3   Add crayfish and shallots. Stir around for 2 minutes.

4   Add cayenne pepper, garlic, tomato, and arugala. Stir around for 1 minute.

5   Add mixed dressing to the pan. Stir around for, at the most, an additional minute. Garnish with cilantro sprigs.

Shrimp Breakfast Stir-Fry

Serves 2 Breakfasts/2 Lunches

PREP   COOK

Scrambled eggs are easy to make in the wok, and a wide variety of ingredients—fresh or leftovers—can be used. Rice, noodles, beans, or veggies taste great in this setting.

1   Cut ingredients into desired sizes.

2   Add a little oil or cooking spray of your choice to the pan. Heat pan to 375°F/medium high heat. Add bacon. Stir around for 1 minute.

3   Add shrimp and bell pepper. Stir around for 2 minutes.

4   Add scallion, rice, and egg mixture. Stir around for 2 minutes.

5   Add a little salt and pepper to taste. Stir for an additional 1 minute. Serve with a slice of wheat or multi-grain bread.

Creole Mixed Seafood Stir-Fry

shopping/to-do list

6 oz. shrimp, peeled and deveined
3 oz. catfish, cut into bite-size pieces
2 andouille sausages, sliced thin
2 celery stalks, chopped
1 small onion, sliced thin
1 green pepper, chopped
1 T garlic, minced
2 okras, sliced thin
salt & pepper to taste
or use Creole seasoning blend to taste
Serve over rice of choice.

Serves 2 Dinners/3 Lunches

PREP   COOK

Creole cuisine is not only native to Louisiana; it is a popular flavor combination using a version of the French "mirepoix." It is called the "Holy Trinity" and includes celery, onions, peppers, and sometimes okra.

1   Cut ingredients into desired sizes.

2   Add a little oil or cooking spray of your choice to the pan. Heat pan to 375°F/medium-high heat.

3   Add shrimp, catfish, and sausages. Stir around for 2 minutes.

4   Add celery, onion, green pepper, garlic, and okra. Stir around for 2 minutes.

5   Add seasonings to taste. Stir around for an additional minute. Serve over rice of choice. (See page 30 for more rice information.)

Indonesian Shrimp Stir-Fry

shopping/to-do list
1 lb. shrimp, peeled and deveined
1 T ginger, fresh grated
1 T garlic, minced
1 hot pepper, chopped finely
1 onion, chopped
1 cup sugar snap peas
¼ cup peanuts, chopped coarsely
1 t sambal or hot sauce
sea salt & pepper to taste
Served with cooked egg noodles.

Serves 2 Dinners/3 Lunches

PREP 0:10   COOK 0:06

Indonesian cuisine is infused with sweet, spicy, and intense flavors, often combined with fruits and nuts like peanuts.

1   Cut ingredients into desired sizes.

2   Add a little oil or cooking spray of your choice to the pan. Heat pan to 375°F/medium-high heat.

3   Add shrimp. Stir around for 2 minutes.

4   Add peas, onion, hot pepper, garlic, and ginger. Stir around for 2 minutes.

5   Add peanuts, sambal to taste, and finish seasoning with a little sea salt and black pepper. Stir around for an additional minute. Serve over cooked egg noodles.

Paella Stir-Fry

Serves 2 Dinners/3 Lunches

```
0:10        0:06
PREP        COOK
```

Paella is a traditional Spanish dish with seafood, fish, mussels, clams, veggies, and rice. Our version is fast and easy to make, and you can add ingredients or omit one, if not available.

shopping/to-do list

8 oz. shrimp, peeled and deveined
4 sausages, cut into bite-size pieces
4 oz. clams or scallops
4 oz. green New Zealand mussels,
defrosted, out of shell
1 bell pepper, or mix of
colored bell peppers, chopped
1 onion, sliced thin
2–3 saffron threads
1 T Spanish paprika powder
2 tomatoes, diced
2 cups yellow rice, cooked al dente
sea salt & pepper to taste
1 T lemon juice

1   Cut ingredients into desired sizes.

2   Add a little oil or cooking spray of your choice to the pan. Heat pan to 375°F/medium-high heat.

3   Add shrimp, sausage, scallops, and mussels. Stir around for 2 minutes.

4   Add bell peppers, onion, saffron, paprika powder, garlic, tomato, and rice. Stir around for 2 minutes.

5   Add lemon juice season with sea salt and pepper to taste. Stir around for an additional minute.

Mixed Shellfish Stir-Fry

Serves 2 Dinners/3 Lunches

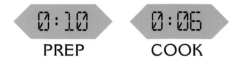

PREP   COOK

A delicious stir-fry of beautiful flavors, this shrimp, lobster, and crayfish dish features lime juice, fruit, and hot sauce. It makes a dramatic, colored dish when served over Forbidden Rice (see page 30).

1   Cut ingredients into desired sizes.

2   Add a little oil or cooking spray of your choice to the pan. Heat pan to 375°F/medium-high heat.

3   Add shellfish. Stir around for 2 minutes.

4   Add mango, star anise, rum, ginger, lime juice, and hot sauce. Stir around for 2 minutes.

5   Season with a little salt and pepper to taste. Serve over Forbidden Rice (see page 30) and garnish with cilantro sprigs.

Mexican Shrimp Stir-Fry

Serves 2 Dinners/3 Lunches

PREP   COOK

Camarones are tiger shrimp caught near the Mexican coast. Shrimp is a great stir-fry ingredient with a built-in thermometer: They turn orange when they're done.

1 Cut ingredients into desired sizes.

2 Add a little oil or cooking spray of your choice to the pan. Heat pan to 375°F/medium-high heat.

3 Add shrimp. Stir around for 2 minutes or until color changes to orange..

4 Add white beans, corn kernels, jalapeño, onion, and garlic.
Stir around for 2 minutes.

5 Add turmeric, parsley, and hot sauce to taste. Stir around for an additional minute. Serve over rice of choice.

Breton Crayfish Stir-Fry

shopping/to-do list

1 cup carrots, sliced
1 small shallot, sliced thin
1 lb. crayfish, peeled and deveined
2 tomatoes, small diced
1 T garlic, minced
1 T fresh chopped parsley
1 T thyme
1 t oregano
1 t lemon juice
1 t coarse black pepper
1 t sea salt
⅓ cup cognac or brandy
Serve over rice, pasta, or potatoes.

Serves 2 Dinners/3 Lunches

0:12 PREP **0:06** COOK

Écrevisses is the French name for crayfish. The Bretons, who live in Bretagne in the northwest of France, prepare them with a rich, flavorful, herbal tomato base and serve the dish with hearty bread.

1 Cut ingredients into desired sizes.

2 Add a little oil or cooking spray of your choice to the pan. Heat pan to 375°F/medium-high heat.

3 Add carrots and shallots. Stir around for 2 minutes.

4 Add crayfish, tomato, garlic, parsley, thyme, oregano, and lemon juice. Stir around for 2 minutes.

5 Add pepper and sea salt to taste. Stir around for an additional minute. Serve with over rice, pasta, or potatoes of choice, and add a nice, mixed green salad.

Lobster Stir-Fry

shopping/to-do list

3–4 lobster tails, cut into bite-size pieces
2 cups asparagus pieces
1 t cayenne pepper
⅓ cup anchovies
½ T curry or turmeric
¼ cup black olives, sliced thin
1 tomato, diced small
1 t paprika
salt and pepper to taste

Serves 2 Dinners/3 Lunches

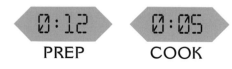

0:12
PREP

0:05
COOK

In the mid 1800's, lobster was "prisoners' food," but because it became more popular, the price of lobsters has increased. For a lobster stir-fry, you do not need a whole lobster. A few lobster tails will do as the main ingredient.

1 Cut ingredients into desired sizes.

2 Add a little oil or cooking spray of your choice to the pan. Heat pan to 375°F/medium-high heat.

3 Add asparagus pieces and stir around for 1 minute.

4 Add lobster, anchovies, cayenne pepper, curry, black olives, and tomato. Stir around for 2 minutes.

5 Add salt, pepper, and paprika to taste. Stir around for an additional minute. Serve with a salad and side dish of choice.

Key West Shrimp Stir-Fry

shopping/to-do list

1 lb. shrimp, peeled and deveined
1 red bell pepper, sliced thin
1 radicchio, sliced
$1/3$ cup pineapple, small cubed
$1/3$ cup watermelon, small cubed
2 T fresh squeezed lime juice
$1/3$ cup coconut, shredded
salt and pepper to taste
Serve over rice or pasta.

Serves 2 Dinners/3 Lunches

| 0:11 | 0:06 |
| PREP | COOK |

Key West is surrounded by oceans filled with an abundance of fresh shrimp, Florida lobster, stone crab, and fish. All ingredients for a great stir-fry dish are available. In addition to the beautiful weather, fresh fruits and coconuts, and great company.

1   Cut ingredients into desired sizes.

2   Add a little oil or cooking spray of your choice to the pan. Heat pan to 375°F/medium high heat.

3   Add shrimp. Stir around for 2 minutes or until color changes to orange.

4   Add bell pepper, radicchio, pineapple, watermelon, and lime juice. Stir around for 2 minutes.

5   Add coconut and season with salt and pepper to taste. Stir around for an additional minute. Serve over rice or pasta.

Sophisticated Crab Stir-Fry

PREP   COOK

The crab meat of choice for our stir-fry recipe is the Chesapeak Bay "jumbo lump" crabmeat. The large, white succulent chunks are delicious and need just a minute or two to heat through.

shopping/to-do list

1 bell pepper, or mix of colored
bell peppers, chopped
1 T ginger, fresh grated
1 T garlic, minced
¼ cup scallions
8 oz. crab meat chunks
1 grapefruit, segments
½ cup champagne (optional)
sea salt & pepper to taste
1 t curry
Garnish with cilantro sprigs.
Serve "as is" over rice or salad.

1   Cut ingredients into desired sizes.

2   Add a little oil or cooking spray of your choice to the pan. Heat pan to 375°F/medium-high heat.

3   Add bell pepper, garlic, ginger, and scallions. Stir around for 2 minutes.

4   Add crab chunks. Stir around for 1 minute.

5   Add grapefruit segments, champagne, and curry and season with a little sea salt and white pepper to taste. Stir around for an additional minute or two. Serve "as is" over rice or on top of a salad.

Sweet & Sour Shrimp Stir-Fry

shopping/to-do list

1 lb. shrimp, peeled and deveined
1 T ginger, fresh grated
1 t lemongrass chopped finely
1 cup bean sprouts
1 t raw sugar
1 t coriander
1 t Worcestershire sauce
2 T soy sauce
Served with rice noodles of choice.

Serves 2 Dinners/3 Lunches

PREP   COOK

Lemongrass is a perennial herb grown in the tropics and subtropics. It is a tall-stemmed, grass-like tropical plant that gives this dish the sour part of "sweet & sour." Lemongrass is also available in cans or jars.

1 Cut ingredients into desired sizes.

2 Add a little oil or cooking spray of your choice to the pan. Heat pan to 375°F/medium high heat.

3 Add shrimp. Stir around for 2 minutes to brown on all sides.

4 Add ginger, lemongrass, and bean sprouts. Stir around for 2 minutes.

5 Add sugar, coriander, Worcestershire, and low sodium soy sauce to taste. Stir around for an additional minute. Serve over rice noodles of choice.

Caribbean Scallop Stir-Fry

shopping/to-do list

8–10 oz. scallops, cut in half
$1/3$ cup salsa
squeeze of lime juice
1 T tarragon
1 red pepper, chopped finely
$1/4$ cup coconut rum
1 t hot sauce
salt & pepper to taste
Serve over brown rice and garnish with
cilantro sprigs.

Serves 2 Dinners/3 Lunches

PREP 0:10   **COOK** 0:06

The scallop comes in two types: sea and bay scallop. The sea scallop is larger in size and has a more nutty flavor than the smaller bay scallop. Scallops freeze well, so you can keep a bag in your freezer for a delicious stir-fry dish.

1 Cut ingredients into desired sizes.

2 Add a little oil or cooking spray of your choice to the pan. Heat pan to 375°F/medium-high heat.

3 Add scallops. Stir around for 2 minutes.

4 Add salsa, lime juice, tarragon, and red pepper. Stir around for 2 minutes.

5 Add rum and hot sauce. Season with a little salt and pepper to taste. Stir around for an additional minute. Serve over brown rice and garnish with cilantro sprigs.

Italian Scallop Stir-Fry

shopping/to-do list

8–10 oz. scallops
1 cup turkey bacon, cut into thin strips
½ cup carrots, julienned
½ cup fava beans
¼ cup pesto
salt and pepper to taste
Serve with pasta and garnish
with a little parmesan cheese.

Serves 2 Dinners/3 Lunches

PREP   COOK

Turkey bacon is a great, lower-fat alternative to regular bacon. It is delicious in combination with scallops and can be served for breakfast, lunch, or dinner.

1   Cut ingredients into desired sizes.

2   Add a little oil or cooking spray of your choice to the pan. Heat pan to 375°F/medium-high heat. Add bacon strips, stir for 1 minute.

3   Add scallops. Stir around for 2 minutes.

4   Add carrot, fava beans, and pesto. Stir around for 2 minutes.

5   Add a little salt and pepper to taste. Stir around for an additional minute. Serve with pasta and garnish with parmesan cheese.

Hawaiian Lobster Stir-Fry

shopping/to-do list

8–10 oz. lobster meat
1 T macadamia nut oil
1 Anaheim pepper, chopped
½ red bell pepper, sliced thin
½ T garlic, minced
½ T ginger, grated
¼ cup seaweed, chopped
⅓ cup coconut milk
salt & pepper to taste
Serve over soaked and drained
rice noodles.

Serves 2 Dinners/3 Lunches

PREP 0:08   **COOK** 0:06

Maine is the largest lobster-producing state in the United States, but did you know that Hawaii also raises fresh Maine lobsters 5,000 miles away from Maine? Lobster is considered a delicacy and is a great stir-fry seafood item.

1   Cut ingredients into desired sizes.

2   Add a little oil or cooking spray of your choice to the pan. Heat pan to 375°F/medium-high heat.

3   Add lobster. Stir around for 2 minutes to brown on all sides.

4   Add peppers, garlic, and ginger. Stir around for 2 minutes.

5   Add seaweed, cayenne pepper, coconut milk, salt, and pepper to taste. Stir around for an additional minute. Serve over soaked and drained rice noodles.

Curried Scallop Stir-Fry

shopping/to-do list

8–10 oz. scallops
1 cup Napa cabbage
1 cup red bell pepper, diced
2 shallots, minced
1 T garlic
2 t turmeric or curry powder
2 T cream or half & half
salt & pepper to taste
Serve over Forbidden Rice.

Serves 2 Dinners/3 Lunches

PREP   COOK

Turmeric is an ancient spice indigenous to southeast Asia. The flavor is warm, aromatic with a slightly bitter undertone; the color is intensely yellow.

1   Cut ingredients into desired sizes.

2   Add a little oil or cooking spray of your choice to the pan. Heat pan to 375°F/medium high heat.

3   Add scallops. Stir around for 2 minutes.

4   Add Napa cabbage, bell pepper, shallots, and garlic. Stir around for 2 minutes.

5   Add turmeric, cream, and season with a little salt and pepper to taste. Stir around for an additional minute. Serve over Forbidden rice. See page 30 for more rice info.

Asian Octopus Stir-Fry Soup

Serves 2 Dinners/3 Lunches

PREP   COOK

Octopus and other seafood like squid, mussels, and shrimp are usually soldseparately but also as a mix, fresh or frozen. A bag of seafood mix in the freezer is always handy when you want to prepare a fast wok lunch or dinner.

1   Cut ingredients into desired sizes.

2   Add a little oil or cooking spray of your choice to the pan. Heat pan to 375°F/medium-high heat.

3   Add seafood. Stir around for 2 minutes.

4   Add tomato, scallions, garlic, and ginger. Stir around for 1 minute.

5   Add red crushed pepper, fish sauce, and stock. Stir around for an additional 2 minutes. Serve with hot sauce on the side.

Chinese Shrimp Stir-Fry

Serves 2 Dinners/3 Lunches

PREP   COOK

Shrimp cooperates with beginner cooksbecause they change color when they are cooked. When pink, they are ready to eat. With our mix of recipes even beginners can be champions in the kitchen.

1 Cut ingredients into desired sizes.

2 Add a little oil or cooking spray of your choice to the pan. Heat pan to 375°F/medium-high heat.

3 Add shrimp. Stir around for 2 minutes.

4 Add broccoli, green beans, fuzzy squash, mushroom, pepper, garlic, and ginger. Stir around for 2 minutes.

5 Add Szechwan pepper and low sodium soy sauce to taste. Stir around for an additional minute. Serve over cooked noodles of choice.

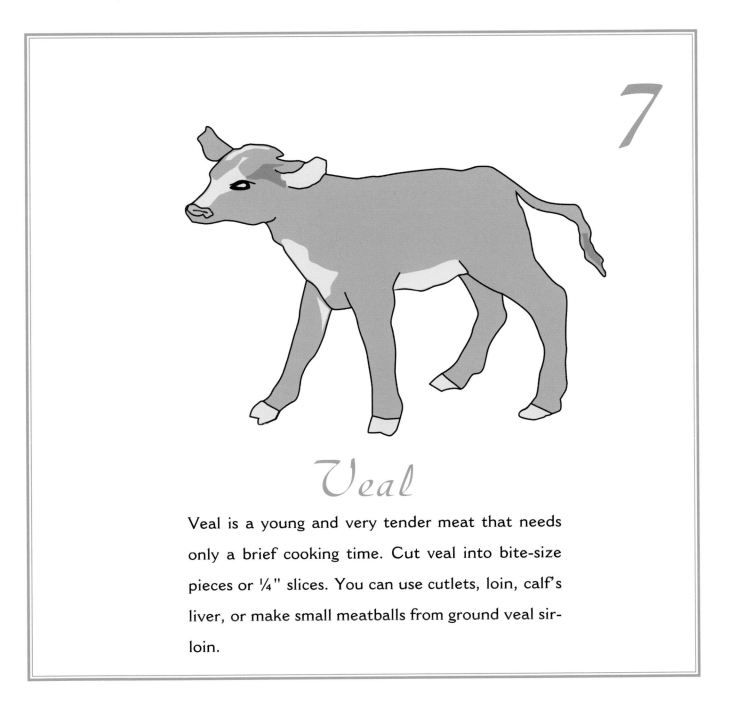

Veal

Veal is a young and very tender meat that needs only a brief cooking time. Cut veal into bite-size pieces or ¼" slices. You can use cutlets, loin, calf's liver, or make small meatballs from ground veal sirloin.

Tuscany Veal Stir-Fry

shopping/to-do list

4 oz. bacon, cut into ¼" pieces
8–12 oz. veal, cut into ½" strips
½ cup leek, sliced
1 cup portobello mushroom, sliced
3 T pesto
1 t red crush pepper
1 T pine nuts
salt & pepper to taste
½ cup white wine
parmesan cheese, grated
Serve over pasta of choice.

Serves 2 Dinners/3 Lunches

PREP | COOK

Veal is a popular meat in Italian cuisine: Veal Scaloppini, Veal Marsala, and Veal Parmigiana are just a few examples of dishes that use it. This stir-fry recipe is a great way to enjoy the bold flavors of Italian cuisine without spending a lot of time in the kitchen.

1   Cut ingredients into desired sizes.

2   Add a little oil or cooking spray of your choice to the pan. Heat pan to 400°F/high heat. Add bacon. Stir around for 1 minute to brown on all sides.

3   Add veal. Stir around for 1 minute to brown on all sides.

4   Add leek, portobello, pesto, red crushed pepper, and pine nuts. Add wine, and a little salt and pepper to taste. Stir around for an additional two minutes. Serve over pasta of choice and sprinkle cheese over the dish.

Gypsy Veal Stir-Fry

shopping/to-do list

8–12 oz. veal, in bite-size pieces
1 shallots, sliced thin
1 yellow bell pepper, diced
1 cup cremini mushrooms, sliced
1 cup tomato, small diced
1 cup white beans
1 T garlic, minced
½ T rosemary
½ T Hungarian paprika
¼ cup red wine
¼ cup half & half or cream
salt & pepper to taste
Serve over rice or potatoes of choice.

Serves 2 Dinners/3 Lunches

0:15
PREP

0:06
COOK

The travels of Gypsies were not limited to the Balkans. There are signs of Gypsies in Egypt, Albania, Hungary, Turkey, England, Germany, Spain, and France, to name just a few. Their cuisine is boldly flavored with lots of fresh herbs and spices.

1   Cut ingredients into desired sizes.

2   Add a little oil or cooking spray of your choice to the pan. Heat pan to 400°F/high heat.

3   Add veal. Stir around for 2 minutes to brown on all sides.

4   Add shallot, bell pepper, mushrooms, tomato, beans, garlic, paprika, and rosemary. Stir around for 2 minutes.

5   Add wine and half & half and season with salt and pepper to taste. Stir around for an additional minute. Serve over rice or potatoes of choice.

Colorful Veal Stir-Fry

shopping/to-do list

8–12 oz. veal, cut into bite-size pieces
2 bell peppers, sliced thin
1 zucchini, sliced thin
1 cup broccoli florets
2 T chives, chopped
1 T garlic
¼ cup marsala (optional)
½ t crushed red pepper
sea salt to taste
Served with any side starch of choice.

Serves 2 Dinners/3 Lunches

PREP   COOK

Veal is a great example of a main ingredient with boundless infusion possibilities. Herbs, spices, and alcoholic flavor agents—like cognac, marsala, madeira, wine, and port—add a beautiful essence to every veal dish.

1   Cut ingredients into desired sizes.

2   Add a little oil or cooking spray of your choice to the pan. Heat pan to 400°F/high heat.

3   Add veal. Stir around for 2 minutes to brown on all sides.

4   Add bell pepper, zucchini, broccoli, chives, and garlic. Stir around for 2 minutes.

5   Add marsala, crushed red pepper, and a little sea salt to taste. Stir around for an additional minute. Serve over any side starch of choice.

Veal & Mushroom Stir-Fry

PREP 0:08   **COOK** 0:06

shopping/to-do list

8–12 oz. veal, cut into bite-size pieces
1 cup mushrooms of choice, sliced
2 scallions, sliced on the bias
1 apple, small diced
1 cup cooked artichokes hearts,
medium diced
1 t cloves, ground
½ T mustard
⅓ cup Madeira (optional)
salt & pepper to taste
Serve with mashed potatoes.
Garnish with basil leaves.

Veal has a neutral flavor that can be used with all five main flavor groups: bitter, sweet, salty, sour, and spicy, so it can be combined with a wide variety of cuisines, styles, and ingredients.

1   Cut ingredients into desired sizes.

2   Add a little oil or cooking spray of your choice to the pan. Heat pan to 400°F/high heat.

3   Add veal. Stir around for 2 minutes to brown on all sides.

4   Add mushroom, scallion, apple, artichoke hearts, and ground cloves. Add mustard, Madeira, and season with a little salt and pepper to taste. Stir around for 2 minutes.

5   Serve with mashed potatoes. Garnish with fresh basil leaves.

Veal Stroganoff Stir-Fry

Serves 2 Dinners/3 Lunches

shopping/to-do list

8–12 oz. veal, cut into bite size pieces
1 small onions, sliced thin
1 green & red bell pepper, cut into
thin strips
2 cups mushrooms, sliced
1 T garlic, minced
1 T tomato paste
½ T black pepper
½ T Hungarian paprika
¼ cup cream or half & half
salt & pepper to taste
Serve over rice, noodles, or potatoes.

0:15 PREP

0:06 COOK

The original Beef Stroganoff is named after a great gourmet, the Russian Count Grigory Stroganove (1770-1857). The original recipe was made with beef, flour, tomato paste, sour cream, broth, onion, and butter, and served over potatoes.

1   Cut ingredients into desired sizes.

2   Add a little oil or cooking spray of your choice to the pan. Heat pan to 400°F/high heat.

3   Add veal. Stir around for 2 minutes to brown on all sides.

4   Add onion, bell pepper, mushroom, and garlic. Stir around for 2 minutes.

5   Add tomato paste, paprika, cream, salt, and pepper to taste. Stir around for an additional minute. Serve over rice or mashed potatoes.

Mediterranean Veal Stir-Fry

Serves 2 Dinners/3 Lunches

`0:08`
PREP

`0:06`
COOK

Veal is used in many southern Mediterranean dishes and served with vegetables du jour (of the day). Our stir-fry recipe infuses bold flavors and tops it with freshly grated Provolone cheese.

1 Cut ingredients into desired sizes.

2 Add a little oil or cooking spray of your choice to the pan. Heat pan to 400°F/high heat.

3 Add veal. Stir around for 2 minutes to brown on all sides.

4 Add cauliflower, mushroom, and garlic. Stir around for 2 minutes.

5 Add artichoke, tomato, peas, and season with salt and pepper to taste. Stir around for an additional minute. Serve over pasta of choice, garnished with grated Provolone cheese.

Veal & Veggie Stir-Fry

8–12 oz. veal, cut into bite-size pieces
1½ cups hard veggies: broccoli,
baby corn, carrots
1 cup soft veggie: string beans, spinach leaves
4 scallions, sliced thin
½ T fresh grated ginger
1 red pepper, finely chopped
a pinch sugar
2 T fish sauce
3 T low sodium soy sauce
2 T freshly squeezed lemon juice
Serve over starch of choice.

Serves 2 Dinners/3 Lunches

PREP   COOK

"When you are a student, you really don't like to cook. So, when you have to, the dishes must be cheap, easy to make, and shouldn't take up a lot of time." This recipe and quote is from my son, Michael Feith.

1   Cut ingredients into desired sizes.

2   Add a little oil or cooking spray of your choice to the pan. Heat pan to 400°F/high heat.

3   Add veal and hard veggies (see page 25). Stir around for 3 minutes to brown on all sides.

4   Add soft veggies, scallion, ginger, red pepper, sugar, fish sauce, soy sauce, and lemon juice. Stir around for an additional minute. Serve over rice or potatoes of choice.

Veal & Arugula Stir-Fry

Serves 2 Dinners/3 Lunches

PREP   COOK

Due to its slightly peppery taste, arugula has the nickname rocket or roquette. Arugula is a bitter, aromatic green with a peppery-mustard flavor.

1   Cut ingredients into desired sizes.

2   Add a little oil or cooking spray of your choice to the pan. Heat pan to 400°F/high heat.

3   Add veal. Stir around for 2 minutes to brown on all sides.

4   Add avocado, garlic, and pecan. Stir around for 2 minutes.

5   Add arugala, lemon juice, wine, and blue cheese and season with salt and pepper to taste. Stir around for an additional minute. Serve with potatoes of choice.

8

Veggies

The gift of "Mother Nature" to us is an abundance of fresh vegetables and fruit that have all the vitamins, minerals, and other nutritional benefits our bodies need every day.

Vibrant Asian Veggie Stir-Fry

Serves 2 Dinners/3 Lunches

PREP   COOK

Vegetables are often called "too bland" or "taste-less," due to old-fashioned hours spent boiling them. When prepared in the wok, the vegetables stay fresh, crisp, and flavorful. This recipe is for the non-believers. Spicy and delicious!

1   Wash veggies and cut them into described sizes.

2   Add a little oil or cooking spray of your choice to the pan. Heat pan to 375°F/medium-high heat.

3   Add bell pepper, carrot, zucchini, and broccoli. Stir around for 2 minutes.

4   Add soybean sprouts, chives, garlic, ginger, scallion, and low sodium soy sauce. Stir around for an additional 2 minutes.

5   Serve over cooked rice and add hot sauce to taste.

Japanese & Napa Cabbage Stir-Fry

shopping/to-do list

6 oz. shiitake mushroom, sliced
2 cups Napa cabbage, sliced
2 cups eggplant, cubed
2 T garlic
2 T ginger
2 T shallots, minced
⅓ cup sake
salt & pepper to taste
1 t wasabi powder
Serve with rice noodles.

Serves 2 Dinners/3 Lunches

0:11 PREP   **0:06** COOK

Cabbage comes in a wide variety of colors, flavors, and names. Napa cabbage is a member of the Chinese cabbage family. It is a good source of vitamin C, folic acid, and fiber. The leaves are white to pale green with frilled edges.

1. Cut ingredients into desired sizes.

2. Add a little oil or cooking spray of your choice to the pan. Heat pan to 375°F/medium-high heat.

3. Add mushroom, cabbage, and eggplant. Stir around for 2 minutes.

4. Add garlic, ginger, and shallot. Season with sake, a little salt, and pepper. Stir around for an additional minute.

5. Serve with rice noodles and a dab of wasabi.

Com Chay Stir-Fry

shopping/to-do list

8 oz. choy chum, sliced
1 small onions, sliced thin
1 green bell pepper, sliced thin
1 T garlic, minced
1 T fresh grated ginger
1/3 cup coconut milk
2 T low sodium soy sauce
2 cups cooked rice

Serves 2 Dinners/3 Lunches

PREP 0:08 COOK 0:05

Com Chay "Buddha Rice" is a Vietnamese vegetarian dish that is traditionally served during the holidays with cooked rice.

1 Cut ingredients into desired sizes.

2 Add a little oil or cooking spray of your choice to the pan. Heat pan to 375°F/medium-high heat.

3 Add choy chum, onion, and bell pepper. Stir around for 2 minutes.

4 Add garlic and ginger. Season with a little pepper. Stir around for 2 minutes.

5 Add coconut milk, soy sauce, and cooked rice. Stir around for an additional minute.

Simply Soy Stir-Fry

Shopping/to do list
8 oz. soy bean sprouts
1 cup edamame
1 cup firm tofu, cubed
1 green hot pepper, chopped
1 T garlic, minced
1 T fresh grated ginger
1 T Szechwan pepper
1 T low sodium soy sauce

Serves 2 Dinners/3 Lunches

PREP 0:10   COOK 0:06

Soybeans contain more protein than other plants, and the protein is of a higher quality, called "complete protein." This means that soybeans and soy products provide all essential amino acids our body needs.

1   Cut ingredients into desired sizes.

2   Add a little oil or cooking spray of your choice to the pan. Heat pan to 375°F/medium-high heat.

3   Add bean sprouts, edamame, tofu, and hot pepper. Stir around for 2 minutes.

4   Add garlic and ginger. Season with a little pepper and soy sauce. Stir around for additional minute.

5   Serve over rice or rice noodles.

Colorful Breakfast Stir-Fry

1 green zucchini, cut into half moons
1 yellow squash, cut into half moons
1 purple eggplant, cut into ¼" cubes
1 bell pepper, color of choice, julienne or mix of colors
1 tomato, small diced
1 T fresh oregano
1 cup eggbeaters or egg whites

Serves 2 Breakfasts

PREP   COOK

The stir-fry technique is ideal for a fast and delicious breakfast. Leftovers from the previous lunch or dinner can be used, with pre-cut and fresh ingredients added.

1   Cut ingredients into desired sizes.

2   Add a little oil or cooking spray of your choice to the pan. Heat pan to 375°F/medium-high heat.

3   Add zucchini, squash, eggplant, and bell pepper. Stir around for 2 minutes.

4   Add tomato and oregano. Stir around for 1 minute.

5   Pour eggs over mixture. Season with a little salt and pepper. Stir around for 2 minutes.

Warm Italian Stir-Fry Salad

shopping/to-do list

8 oz. mixed greens
1 cup spinach
⅓ cup eggplant, cubed
1 T garlic, minced
¼ cup basil, chiffonade
1 T oregano, chopped
salt & pepper to taste
2 T Provolone cheese, grated

dressing:

4 T balsamic vinegar
2 T olive oil
1 T Italian seasoning

Serves 2 Dinners/3 Lunches

PREP   COOK

Warm salads are satisfying, easy to make, and unlimited in possibilities and flavor combinations. Here is an example with Italian flavors and herbs.

1 Cut ingredients into desired sizes.

2 Add a little oil or cooking spray of your choice to the pan. Heat pan to 375°F/medium-high heat.

3 Add eggplant, garlic, and oregano. Stir around for 2 minutes.

4 Add spinach, basil, and mixed greens. Season with little salt and pepper. Stir around for 1 minute.

5 Mix vinegar and olive oil with Italian seasoning and add to pan. Stir around for an additional minute.

Japanese Tofu Stir-Fry

shopping/to-do list

8–12 oz. firm tofu, ¼" cubed
1 T garlic, minced
1 T fresh grated ginger
3 T scallions, sliced on the bias
½ cup shiitake mushrooms, sliced
¼ cup sake
2 T black sesame seeds, toasted
⅓ cup low sodium soy sauce
a pinch of sugar
1 t red crushed pepper
Serve with noodles of choice.

Serves 2 Dinners/3 Lunches

0:08 PREP   0:05 COOK

Tofu is soybean curd, made by treating heated soy milk with a coagulant to produce curds. The curds can be pressed to different firmness of tofu: soft for soups and regular and firm for sautéing and stir-fries.

1   Cut ingredients into desired sizes.

2   Add a little oil or cooking spray of your choice to the pan. Heat pan to 375°F/medium-high heat.

3   Add scallion, ginger, and garlic. Stir around for 30 seconds.

4   Add tofu, mushroom, soy sauce, and pinch of sugar. Stir around for 2 minutes.

5   Serve over noodles and garnish with black sesame seeds and red crushed pepper.

Colorful Tofu Stir-Fry

Serves 2 Dinners/3 Lunches

PREP   COOK

Tofu has a bland taste, but when infused with other ingredients, it has the quality—like a chameleon—to adjust itself to the flavors of the infusions.

1   Cut ingredients into desired sizes.

2   Add a little oil or cooking spray of your choice to the pan. Heat pan to 375°F/medium-high heat.

3   Add bell pepper, leek, and bean sprouts. Stir around for 30 seconds.

4   Add tofu, stir-fry seasoning, and soy sauce to taste. Stir around for 2 minutes.

5   Serve "as is" or over rice or noodles.

Badhinjan Buran Stir-Fry

shopping/to-do list

8 oz. eggplant, small diced
1 cup carrots, sliced
1 cup celery, sliced
1 red bell pepper, chopped
1 T garlic, minced
salt & pepper to taste
3 T spicy yogurt sauce
1/8 cup goat cheese
Serve with tomato and cucumber salad.

Serves 2 Dinners/3 Lunches

PREP   COOK

Badhinjan Buran, which means "Princess Buran's eggplant," is an Arabic dish with its main ingredient (eggplant) prepared with yogurt and spices.

1   Cut ingredients into desired sizes.

2   Add a little oil or cooking spray of your choice to the pan. Heat pan to 375°F/medium-high heat.

3   Add eggplant, carrot, celery, and bell pepper. Stir around for 2 minutes.

4   Add garlic, and season with a little salt and pepper to taste. Stir around for 2 minutes.

5   Serve with a tomato and cucumber salad, crumbled goat cheese, and spicy yogurt sauce (see page 230). Garnish with mint leaves.

Brown Striped Tofu Stir-Fry

shopping/to-do list

1 cup mixed bell pepper diced
1/3 cup shallots, sliced on the bias
8 oz. brown tofu, striped
1 cup chinese mushrooms
2 T garlic, minced
1 T fresh ginger, minced
1/3 cup sake or vegetable stock
1 T white pepper
1 T low sodium soy sauce

Serves 2 Dinners/3 Lunches

PREP   COOK

*Brown striped tofu is a fried tofu that pro-
vides a contrast in this colorful dish. Striped
tofu, cooked noodles, and pan-fried noodles are
available in the chilled produce section of your
grocery store.*

1   Cut ingredients into desired sizes.

2   Add a little oil or cooking spray of your choice to the pan. Heat pan to
    375°F/medium-high heat.

3   Add bell pepper and shallot. Stir around for 2 minutes.

4   Add tofu, mushroom, garlic, and ginger. Season with a little pepper.
    Stir around for 2 minutes.

5   Add sake and soy sauce. Stir around for an additional minute.

Italian Veggie Stir-Fry

Serves 2 Dinners/3 Lunches

PREP   COOK

Italy is known for pasta, tomato sauce, olive oil, and fresh herbs. This recipe has everything indigenous to the rich Italian kitchen, but prepared in only 4 minutes cooking time.

1   Cut ingredients into desired sizes.

2   Add a little oil or cooking spray of your choice to the pan. Heat pan to 375°F/medium-high heat.

3   Add eggplant, fava beans, spinach, and tomato. Stir around for 2 minutes.

4   Add garlic, olives, oregano, and wine vinegar. Season with a little salt and pepper to taste. Stir around for an additional minute.

Summer Ratatouille Stir-Fry

shopping/to-do list

1 eggplant, cut into small cubs
1 yellow and 1 green squash, sliced and cut into
half moons
1 onion, sliced thin
1 cucumber, sliced thin and cut into
half moons
1 T garlic, minced
1 cup orange, segments
2 T pine nuts
1 T herbs de provence
salt & pepper to taste
Serve with roasted pearl potatoes and
garnish with parsley.

Serves 2 Dinners/3 Lunches

PREP   COOK

Ratatouille is a recipe indigenous to Provence, prepared with an abundance of fresh produce, like tomatoes, eggplant, zucchini, and bell pepper. Summer ratatouille can be served warm, or refreshingly chilled in the summer.

1   Cut ingredients into desired sizes.

2   Add a little oil or cooking spray of your choice to the pan. Heat pan to 375°F/medium-high heat.

3   Add eggplant, squash, onion, cucumber, and garlic. Stir around for 2 minutes.

4   Add orange segments, pine nuts, and Herbs de Provence. Season with a little sea salt and white pepper. Stir around for an additional minute.

5   Serve with roasted pearl potatoes, and garnish with parsley.

Worldly Eggplant Stir-Fry

shopping/to-do list

1 white eggplant, diced small
1 purple eggplant, diced small
3 Thai eggplant, diced small
1 Brazilian eggplant, diced small
1 cup mushroom, sliced
2 T pesto
salt & pepper to taste
Serve over rice, pasta, or
couscous of choice.

Serves 2 Dinners/3 Lunches

PREP COOK

Eggplant are also called "aubergine."
They come in different shapes and colors:
Italian—purple, thin skin; Thai—light green
with dark stripes Brazilian—orange and pastel
colored, white, white lavender stripes, purple
with white.

1   Cut ingredients into desired sizes.

2   Add a little oil or cooking spray of your choice to the pan. Heat pan to 375°F/medium-high heat.

3   Add all eggplant dices. Stir around for 2 minutes.

4   Add mushroom and pesto and season with a little salt and pepper. Stir around for 2 minutes.

5   Serve over rice, pasta, or couscous of choice. Garnish with a tomato or hot sauce and thyme sprigs or mint leaves.

Catalan Spinach Stir-Fry

Serves 2 Dinners/3 Lunches

PREP   COOK

Catalan is a beautiful province in the north-east of Spain, touching the Pyrenees and the Mediterranean coastline. Barcelona is its largest city, with an ancient history and culinary wealth.

1   Cut ingredients into desired sizes.

2   Add a little oil or cooking spray of your choice to the pan. Heat pan to 375°F/medium high heat.

3   Add shallot, bell pepper, garlic, and raisins. Stir around for 2 minutes.

4   Add spinach. Season with a little pepper and sea salt. Stir around for 2 minutes. Serve over rice of choice.

Indonesian Mushroom Stir-Fry

shopping/to-do list

2 cups mushrooms, sliced
2 cups cabbage, sliced
1 cucumber, do not peel, cut in half moons
1 onion, sliced thin
1 cup bean sprouts
a little salt & pepper to taste
1 t cumin
1 t sugar
2 T ketjap manis (sweet soy sauce)
½ t sambal oelek
Serve with bahmi or other egg noodles.

Serves 2 Dinners/3 Lunches

0:15 PREP   0:04 COOK

Indonesian cuisine combines sweet and intense flavors. Sambal (Indonesian hot sauce) is made at different levels of heat and flavor. A pinch of sambal often adds a sufficient amount of heat.

1   Cut ingredients into desired sizes.

2   Add a little oil or cooking spray of your choice to the pan. Heat pan to 375°F/medium-high heat.

3   Add mushroom, cabbage, cucumber, onion, and bean sprouts. Stir around for 2 minutes.

4   Add cumin, sugar, ketjap, and sambal. Season with a little salt and pepper. Stir around for an additional minute.

5   Serve with bahmi or other type of egg noodles.

Simply Mushroom Stir-Fry

Serves 2 Dinner/3 Lunches

0:15 PREP   **0:06** COOK

Mushroom are fungi that have—according to ancient history—health benefits that help strengthen our immune system and help our body fight cancer and cardiovascular diseases by lowering blood pressure.

1 Cut ingredients into desired sizes.

2 Add a little oil or cooking spray of your choice to the pan. Heat pan to 375°F/medium-high heat.

3 Add all mushrooms and chives. Stir around for 2 minutes.

4 Add garlic and marsala. Season with a little salt and pepper. Stir around for an additional minute. Garnish with chopped chives and 2–3 flower tops.

5 Serve with rice or couscous of choice.

Spanish Green Bean Stir-Fry

shopping/to-do list

2 cups green beans
1 cup tomatoes, diced
½ cup black olives, sliced
1 Spanish onion, diced
1 T garlic, minced
1 t Spanish paprika powder
1 cup red wine (optional)
salt & pepper to taste
Serve over rice of choice.

Serves 2 Dinners/3 Lunches

PREP   COOK

Colorful, delicious, flavorful, and with an abundance of healthy ingredients. That is the simple rule of Spanish cooking.

1   Cut ingredients into desired sizes.

2   Add a little oil or cooking spray of your choice to the pan. Heat pan to 375°F/medium-high heat.

3   Add green beans, tomato, olives, and onion. Stir around for 2 minutes.

4   Add garlic, paprika, and red wine. Season with a little sea salt and pepper. Stir around for an additional minute.

5   Serve over rice of choice.

Hearts of Palm Stir-Fry

shopping/to-do list

8 oz. hearts of palm, sliced
4 oz. shiitake mushroom, sliced
1 shallot, minced
1 bell pepper, diced
1 T coconut milk
salt & pepper to taste
Serve as side dish or "as is."

Serves 2 Dinners/3 Lunches

0:15 PREP   **0:06** COOK

Hearts of palm are the heart of the Sabal Palmetto, a tough-barked palm that is grown in Florida and South America. The entire palm heart is rarely available fresh, but is available canned. Its smooth off-white colored flesh is velvety.

1   Cut ingredients into desired sizes.

2   Add a little oil or cooking spray of your choice to the pan. Heat pan to 375°F/medium-high heat.

3   Add hearts of palm, mushroom, shallot, and bell pepper. Stir around for 2 minutes.

4   Add coconut milk and season with a little salt and pepper.
Stir around for an additional minute.

5   Serve as side dish or "as is."

9

Desserts

The stir-fry technique is ideal for preparing a fruit dessert because it's fast and doesn't destroy the fruit's soft texture.

Colorful Mixed Berry Stir-Fry

shopping/to-do list

1 cup raspberries
1 cup blueberries
1 cup blackberries
1 cup strawberries, sliced
$\frac{1}{3}$ cup mint leaves
1 t lemon juice
a pinch of sugar
$\frac{1}{3}$ cup cognac
Served with frozen yogurt, garnish with mint leaves and a lemon meringue.

Serves 2–4 Desserts

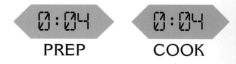

PREP   COOK

Berries come in a wide variety: blueberries, cranberries, currants, gooseberries, elderberries, raspberries, saskatoons, and strawberries. Choose berries that are in season for optimal flavor and to keep an eye on your budget.

1   Cut ingredients into desired sizes.

2   Add a little hazelnut or walnut oil to the pan. Heat pan to 325°F/medium heat.

3   Add fruit. Stir around for 1 minute.

4   Add lemon juice, sugar, and cognac. Stir around for an additional minute or two.

5   Serve with frozen yogurt, and garnish with mint leaves and a lemon meringue.

Gingered Peach Stir-Fry

shopping/to-do list

4 cups peaches, sliced
2 T crystallized ginger, chopped
2 T hazelnuts, coarsely chopped
2 T maple syrup
1 t vanilla extract
$1/3$ cup cognac
Serve over chocolate ice cream.

Serves 2–4 Desserts

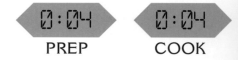

PREP   COOK

Crystallized ginger complements the sweet freshness of peaches, and the sweetness of chocolate ice cream turns this dessert into a real feast.

1   Cut ingredients into desired sizes.

2   Add a little hazelnut or walnut oil to the pan. Heat pan to 325°F/medium heat.

3   Add fruit. Stir around for 2 minutes.

4   Add ginger and hazelnuts. Stir around for one minute.

5   Add maple syrup, vanilla extract, and cognac. Stir around for an additional minute. Serve over chocolate ice cream.

Warm Fruit Salad Stir-Fry

shopping/to-do list
8–10 oz. of mixed fruit:
kiwi (peeled, sliced), papaya (peeled, cubed), currants, passion fruit (flesh scooped out of shell), watermelon (peeled, cubed), grapes, strawberries (quartered)
1/3 cup Cointreau (alternative: apple juice)
a squeeze of lemon juice
a pinch of raw sugar
Garnish with mint leaves.

Serves 2–4 Desserts

PREP 0:10   COOK 0:04

Warm fruit tastes even better than cold fruit because the flavors intensify, and, when combined, the flavors even "marry" and "complement" each other. In plain English: it's just delicious!

1 Cut ingredients into desired sizes.

2 Add a little hazelnut or walnut oil to the pan. Heat pan to 325°F/medium heat.

3 Add all fruit. Stir around for 2 minutes.

4 Add Cointreau, squeezed lemon juice, and a pinch of sugar. Stir around for an additional minute.

5 Serve "as is" or top with whipped cream or Cool Whip and garnish with mint leaves.

Dutch "Boeren Jongens" Stir-Fry

Serves 2–4 Desserts

PREP   COOK

Dutch "Boeren Jongens" (Farmers Boys) is a traditional recipe served at birthday parties with whipped cream. The ingredients are also the base for "Boeren Jongens" ice cream. Our version is prepared in the wok and served with a Dutch pancake.

1   Cut ingredients into desired sizes.

2   Add a little hazelnut or walnut oil to the pan. Heat pan to 325°F/medium heat.

3   Add apples, walnut, and raisins. Stir around for 2 minutes.

4   Add brandy. Stir around for an additional 1 minute.

5   Serve with Dutch pancakes (French crepes) and top with whipped cream.

Simply Pear Stir-Fry

Serves 2–4 Desserts

PREP   COOK

Pears served warm are very popular in the "old comfort cuisine," and they are often poached with a variety of liquors. This stir-fry version is delicious—warm pears combined with pecans and the tart taste of currants.

1   Cut ingredients into desired sizes.

2   Add a little hazelnut or walnut oil to the pan. Heat pan to 325°F/medium heat.

3   Add pears. Stir around for 1 to 2 minutes.

4   Add currants, nutmeg, and cinnamon. Stir around for an additional minute.

5   Serve with ice cream and a tuille cookie.

Warm Apple Stir-Fry

shopping/to-do list

4 cups apple, sliced
¼ cup walnuts, chopped coarsely
¼ cup raisins
1 t sugar
1 t cinnamon
Serve with frozen yogurt.

Serves 2–4 Desserts

PREP   COOK

Warm apples with cinnamon and raisins are the base for many delicious desserts, like pies or strudel. This wok version gives a new dimension to frozen yogurt.

1   Cut ingredients into desired sizes.

2   Add a little hazelnut or walnut oil to the pan. Heat pan to 325°F/medium heat.

3   Add apples. Stir around for 2 minutes.

4   Add walnuts, raisins, sugar, and cinnamon. Stir around for an additional minute.

5   Serve with frozen yogurt.

Orange Pecan Stir-Fry

shopping/to-do list

3 oranges, segments cut in half
½ cup pecan pieces
1 T brown sugar
⅓ cup butterscotch chips
⅓ cup rum
Serve over ice cream of choice.

Serves 2–4 Desserts

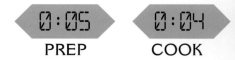

PREP   COOK

The stir-fry technique is ideal for heating up fruit because it's fast and doesn't destroy the soft texture.

1   Cut ingredients into desired sizes.

2   Add a little hazelnut or walnut oil to the pan. Heat pan to 325°F/medium heat.

3   Add oranges. Stir around for 2 minutes.

4   Add pecans, sugar, butterscotch chips, and rum. Stir around for 2 minutes.

5   Serve over ice cream of choice.

Apricot Pistachios Stir-Fry

Serves 2–4 Desserts

0:10 PREP

0:04 COOK

Dried fruit is easy to re-hydrate in water, or for additional flavor, soak in a liquor of choice. When using liquor, reserve the soaking liquid to add later.

shopping/to-do list
2 cups apricots, soaked for ± 10 minutes in
water or Cointreau, drain but
save the liquid
½ cup pistachios
1 t vanilla extract
1 T maple syrup
Serve warm over French vanilla ice cream or
frozen yogurt.

1   Cut ingredients into desired sizes.

2   Add little hazelnut or walnut oil to the pan. Heat pan to 325°F/medium heat.

3   Add apricots. Stir around for 2 minutes.

4   Add pistachios, vanilla extract, and maple syrup. Stir around for an additional minute.

5   Serve warm over French vanilla ice cream or frozen yogurt.

Caribbean Fruit Stir-Fry

Serves 2–4 Desserts

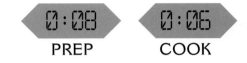

PREP 0:08 **COOK** 0:06

The colorful culture and cuisine of the Caribbean combines tartness and sweetness of a wide variety of fruit. The bold flavors intensify during the stir-fry preparation.

1 Cut ingredients into desired sizes.

2 Add a little hazelnut or walnut oil to the pan. Heat pan to 325°F/medium heat.

3 Add fruit. Stir around for 2 minutes.

4 Add lime juice, sugar, and rum. Stir around for an additional minute.

5 Serve "as is" or with ice cream.

Coconut Cherries Stir-Fry

Serves 2–4 Desserts

PREP   COOK

Coconut gives an exotic, rich flavor infusion to the slightly tart flavor of cherries. Fresh cherries are great to use when in season, but it is a bit of a task to remove the pits, so using canned cherries is a good alternative.

1 Prepare ingredients as described in the shopping list.

2 Add little hazelnut or walnut oil to the pan. Heat pan to 325°F/medium heat.

3 Add cherries. Stir around for 2 minutes.

4 Add sugar, lemon juice, ½ cup of coconut, nutmeg, and brandy. Stir around for an additional 2 minutes.

5 Serve over frozen yogurt in a chocolate cup, garnished with the tablespoon of coconut and a few basil or mint leaves.

Pomegranate Stir-Fry

shopping/to-do list

2 bananas, sliced
¼ cup pomegranate juice
¼ cup Grand Marnier (optional)
2 T almond slivers
⅓ cup basil, chiffonade
Serve with frozen vanilla yogurt.

Serves 2–4 Desserts

0:05
PREP

0:03
COOK

Inside the vibrant red skin of the pomegranate, you'll find arils, delicious sacks of juice that surround the seeds. Check www.pomwonderful.com for delicious recipes using this 5,000 year old fruit.

1   Cut ingredients into desired sizes.

2   Add a little hazelnut or walnut oil to the pan. Heat pan to 325°F/medium heat.

3   Add bananas and pomegranate juice. Stir around for 1 minute.

4   Add basil and Grand Marnier. Stir around for an additional minute.

5   Serve with frozen vanilla yogurt, and garnish with almond slivers.

Bananas Foster Stir-Fry

Serves 2–4 Desserts

PREP   COOK

The stir-fry technique is ideal for this old-fashioned recipe, created in New Orleans but known all over the country. Flambée or just heat and serve.

1   Cut ingredients into desired sizes.

2   Add a little hazelnut or walnut oil to the pan. Heat pan to 325°F/medium heat.

3   Add bananas. Stir around for 1 minute.

4   Add shredded coconut, coconut milk, and rum. Stir around for an additional minute.

5   Serve with vanilla ice cream and whipped cream.

Sauces, Soups & Seasonings

Soups, sauces, and dressings have a bold flavor when fresh herbs and freshly ground spices are used. A hearty cup of soup is a great appetizer, lunch, or snack on a cold, rainy day. A tangy, amazingly refreshing fruit-infused dressing with the savor of the Caribbean turns a regular salad into a tropical delight or provides your stir-fry with unlimited flavor combinations and possibilities

Soy Stir-Fry Sauce

shopping/to-do list

3 cups low sodium soy sauce
½ cup pineapple, chopped finely
1 T ginger, grated
1 T garlic, minced
1 t sugar in the raw
1 T lime juice

0:08 PREP   **0:05** COOK

1   Cut ingredients into described sizes.

2   Add a little oil to the pan. Heat pan to 375°F/medium-high heat.

3   Add ingredients. Stir around for 4 minutes.

4   Serve with beef, pork, poultry, or ice cream.

Fruity Stir-Fry Sauce

shopping/to-do list

3 cups papaya, diced
1 T ginger, fresh grated
1 cup cream of coconut
½ t cayenne powder
⅓ cup rum (optional)

0:08 PREP   **0:05** COOK

1   Cut ingredients into described sizes.

2   Add a little oil to the pan. Heat pan to 375°F/medium-high heat.

3   Add ingredients. Stir around for 4 minutes.

4   Serve with beef, poultry, or ice cream.

Indonesian Peanut Sauce

shopping/to-do list

1 cup plain peanuts
⅓ cup vegetable oil
or 1 cup peanut butter
3 T garlic, minced
1 t sambal or hot sauce
1 t brown sugar
2 T ketjap or dark soy sauce

0:03 PREP **0:11** COOK

1. Add a little oil to the pan. Heat pan to 375°F/medium-high heat. When hot, add peanuts. Stir around for ± 4 minutes.

2. Remove from pan, place on paper towel to drain, and place in blender until blended well. Pour off oil, but do not clean the pan. Re-heat pan and add garlic, sambal, sugar, and ketjap. Stir around for 2 minutes.

3. Add peanut mixture and stir around for 5 minutes. Serve with meat or veggies.

Papaya Sauce

shopping/to-do list

3 cups papaya, diced small
1 T ginger, fresh grated
1 cup coconut cream
½ t cayenne powder
⅓ cup rum (optional)

0:08 PREP **0:05** COOK

1. Cut ingredients into described sizes.

2. Add a little oil to the pan. Heat pan to 375°F/medium-high heat.

3. Add ingredients. Stir around for 4 minutes.

4. Serve with beef, poultry, or ice cream.

Fruity Salad Dressing

0:08 PREP   0:05 COOK

1   Cut ingredients into described sizes.

2   Juice the fruit or use store-bought fresh juice (no sugar added). Add rest of ingredients. Mix well.

3   Keep refrigerated for a few days in an air-tight jar.

Warm Salad Dressing

0:08 PREP   0:05 COOK

1   Cut ingredients into described sizes.

2   Add a little oil to the pan. Heat pan to 375°F/medium-high heat.

3   Add rest of the ingredients. Stir around for 4 minutes.

4   Serve over a peppery, mixed green salad.

shopping/to-do list

3 cups peaches, small diced
1 t hazelnut oil
2 T basil, fresh chopped
½ cup brandy
1 t sugar in the raw
1 T lime juice
⅓ cup pecans, chopped

Warm Peach Chutney

0:08 PREP   **0:05** COOK

1   Cut ingredients into described cuts.

2   Add a little oil to the pan. Heat pan to 375°F/medium-high heat.

3   Add ingredients. Stir around for 4 minutes.

4   Serve with beef, pork, poultry, or try it with a scoop of vanilla ice cream.

---

shopping/to-do list

1 T olive oil
3 cups carrots juice
1 T ginger, fresh grated
⅓ cup red wine vinegar
⅔ cup extra virgin olive oil
sea salt & ground black pepper to taste

Carrot Ginger Sauce

0:11 PREP   **0:05** COOK

1   Cut ingredients into described sizes.

2   Add a little oil to the pan. Heat pan to 375°F/medium-high heat.

3   Add ingredients. Stir around for 4 minutes.

4   Serve warm with beef, pork, poultry, or chilled over a salad.

Garlic Yogurt Sauce

0:07 PREP   **0:03** COOK

1   Mix all ingredients. Mix well.

2   Add ground cloves and cinnamon. *For spicy version:* add 1 t cayenne.

3   Yogurt sauces match well with grilled vegetables, cucumber salads, North African, and curried dishes.

Thai King Do Sauce

0:10 PREP   **0:05** COOK

1   Place softened fruit in blender. Blend well.

2   Add a little oil to the pan. Heat pan to 375°F/medium-high heat.

3   Add all ingredients. Stir around for 4 minutes.

4   Serve this spicy sauce with meat of choice.

Easy Miso Soup

0:03 PREP   **0:03** COOK

1   Cut ingredients into described sizes.

2   Bring water to a boil. Add scallions and miso paste. Turn heat down, stir around for 2 minutes.

3   Add tofu, nori, and soy sauce. Stir for an additional minute.

Dashi Soup

0:08 PREP   **0:05** COOK

1   Cut ingredients into described cuts.

2   Bring water to a boil. Add dashi and bring back to a boil.

3   Add shrimp, veggies, tofu, and ginger. Stir around for 2 minutes.

4   Add nori. Stir for an additional minute.

Black Bean Soup

0:25 PREP   **1:00** COOK

shopping/to-do list

1 T olive oil
2 lb. ground chicken, beef, or a
mix of ground meat
1 sweet onion, sliced
10 green onions, cut in ½" pieces
1 banana pepper or 2 smaller size Caribbean peppers, medium diced
1 hot pepper (for example: jalapeño, Cubanelle),
medium diced
2 bell peppers (mix of red, orange or green), medium diced
3 T Mexican spice blend
3 lb. of dried black beans (soaked overnight) or 6
cans of black beans, rinsed and drained
± 1½–2 qt. of stock, or more
if needed
3 T garlic, minced
10 oz. carrots, shredded
15 oz. corn kernels
6 tomatoes, medium size
medium diced cilantro
tortilla chips

This hearty soup is full of vegetables and is light and spicy with peppers and tomatoes. Makes a great meal served with chips, salsa, or a salad with avocados. Servings: ± twenty 15 oz. storage containers, which form a great inventory of frozen soup together with the Chicken & Veggie Soup from page 233.

1. Cut ingredients into described sizes. Heat oil in large stock pot. Add meat to brown lightly. Add onions, peppers, bell peppers, stir around for a few minutes.

2. Add Mexican spice blend, black beans, and stock. Bring to a boil and let simmer for a few minutes.

3. Add garlic, carrots, and corn kernels. Simmer covered for 30 minutes. Stir at least every 10 minutes.

4. Add tomatoes and let simmer 15 more minutes. Serve with freshly chopped cilantro, and tortilla chips, and a little bit of hot sauce to taste.

Chicken & Veggie Soup

0:25	1:00
PREP	COOK

By making these soups when you have a spare moment and freezing them in meal-size containers, you will have a healthy meal the next time you don't have time to cook. Build an inventory of soups that will comfort your cravings and satisfy your nutritional needs in all seasons.

1   Cut ingredients into described cuts. Place in stockpot with enough water to cover the chicken completely. Place bouquet garni and sachet d'épice (see spice blends page 234) and bring to a rapid boil.

2   Let simmer until meat falls apart (± 45 minutes). Skim the scum (foam on top of surface).

3   In sauté pan or wok, heat up a little oil. Stir onion, carrots, potatoes, and garlic around for a few minutes.

4   Boil tomatoes for ± 10 minutes and place in food mill or blender to puree. Add veggie mix, tomatoes, and seasoning. Bring all to a boil. Let simmer for ± 10 minutes. Adjust seasoning as needed.

5   Store in refrigerator for ± 4–5 days or in freezer for ± 1 month.

Create Your Own Spice Blend

We give you a few examples of spice blends. The charts on pages 18 and 19 show which spices and herbs are indigenous to different cuisines:

Cajun—a blend of allspice, bay leaf, cloves, garlic, salt, onion, paprika, oregano, red crushed pepper, thyme, white pepper

Caribbean—black pepper, cumin seed (freshly ground), fennel, oregano, red crushed pepper, sea salt

French Herbes de Provence—fennel seeds (freshly ground), marjoram, rosemary, sage, summer savory, thyme, young lavender

Hawaiian—black pepper, cardamom, coriander, cumin, garlic, ginger, sea salt, turmeric.

Hungarian—basil, black pepper, mace, lavender, paprika, thyme

Indian Curry—cardamom, cayenne, cinnamon, cloves, coriander, cumin seeds (freshly ground), garam masala, ginger powder, mustard seeds (freshly ground), nutmeg, onion, pepper, turmeric

Indonesian—chervil, chives, coriander, ginger, chopped lemongrass, marjoram, oregano.

Italian—basil, chives, garlic, hyssop, lavender, oregano, parsley, savory, thyme

Magreb (North African)—cinnamon, coriander seeds (freshly ground) cumin seeds (freshly ground), fenugreek, lemon zest

Mediterranean—basil, black pepper, ground cloves, nutmeg, parsley, sea salt, spearmint, sumac, young lavender

Mexican—cilantro (dried), coriander seeds (freshly ground), cumin seeds (freshly ground) lime zest, oregano, red crushed pepper

Thai—cardamom, coriander seeds (freshly ground) red crushed pepper, sesame seeds, turmeric

The Benefit of Marinating

The benefit of marinating is to infuse the flavor combinations of the marinade into the food by immersing the food in a liquid/herb/spice-mix. Another purpose of a marinade is to tenderize meat.

Most marinades contain an acid ingredient, so do not use an aluminum bowl. Use a glass or ceramic one and place the marinated item in the refrigerator during the marinating time.

The components of a marinade:

1. Acid: citrus juice, vinegar, wine (red, white, or mirin)
2. Spices: see chart on page 18 and 19
3. Herbs: see intro pages
4. Flavor enhancers: hot peppers, fresh roots: garlic, ginger, etc.

Immerse the meat in the marinade for at least 2 hours. For tenderizing meat, let it marinate overnight for the best result. Many marinades are available in many flavor combinations from all over the world. Check the label for the sodium content to prevent over-seasoning. Lemon and lime are bolder citrus types that leave a strong citrus flavor. If desired you can choose orange juice and orange zest. Like with everything in life, be creative and try some different flavor combinations.

Wok Temperatures & Oil

Before adding oil to the pan, the pan should be heated to the correct temperature:

400°F Meat, poultry, hard veggies

375°F Fish, seafood, soft veggies, sauces and dressings

325°F Desserts

The smoke point of oil is the temperature at which the oil starts to decompose and starts to smoke. The "breakdown" of the oil creates a repugnant smell. For the best result in stir-fry cooking, use refined oil. A few examples:

Refined Oils	Usage	Smoke Point
Almond oil	cold/low temp	SP 495°F
Avocado oil	all purpose	SP 520°F
Canola (rapeseed) oil	all purpose	SP 400°F
Corn oil	all purpose	SP 450°F
Extra virgin olive oil	cold/low temp	SP 406°F
Hazelnut oil	all purpose	SP 482°F
Olive oil	all purpose	SP 468°F
Grape seed	cold/low temp	SP 400°F
Peanut (arachide oil)	all purpose	SP 450°F
Safflower, high oleic	all purpose	SP 450°F
Soybean	all purpose	SP 450°F
Sunflower seed oil	all purpose	SP 450°F
Sesame oil	all purpose	SP 410°F
Vegetable oil (blend)	all purpose	SP 400–475°F
Walnut oil	cold/low temp	SP 495°F

Oil Infusion

Blanch herbal leaves of choice
in boiling water for 2 minutes.
Squeeze to remove water;
place in blender and add oil of choice.
Keep chilled in the refrigerator.
Remember, a little goes a long way.

Oils Best for Stir-Fries

Remember that a little oil goes a long way. Pouring oil into an oil-sprayer is a great way to control the amount of oil you need to use. Use unsaturated fats, which help lower cholesterol. A few examples of oils suitable for stir-fries are:

Avocado oil—A smooth oil with a rich, but not overpowering flavor.

Canola oil—This oil has the benefit of being more cholesterol-balancing than other oil.

Hazelnut oil—This oil contain 93 percent unsaturated fat, which makes it one of the healthiest fats.

Olive oil—Especially great to use for veggies. Adds a slight olive flavor to your stir-fry.

Peanut oil—Traditionally used in Asian cuisine, also called arachide oil. Thicker than most oils, with a distinguished flavor.

Sesame oil—Another example of a traditional Asian oil, but great for many other cuisines.

Soybean oil—The extract of soybeans. This oil does not contain any cholesterol but has linoleic acid, which is an omega-3 fatty acid, that helps prevent cardiovascular diseases.

Kikkoman and Amoy also sell flavored oils for stir-fry. Check your international food aisle at your grocery store.

Stir-Fry Ingredients of the World

These are the most popular flavoring agents and additions to make your stir-fries, soups, and sauces the healthiest and the best!

Amoy—One of the great companies that makes stir-fry sauces, sateh sauce, soy sauces, and great flavor-enhancers.

Baby corn—Canned baby corn can be used in all types of cuisines.

Bamboo shoots—A member of the grass family, low in calories and fat. They are crisp and add great flavor to your stir-fry.

Black bean sauce—This thick, dark brown sauce is made of fermented black beans.

Chinese soy sauce—The thickest type of soy sauce, darker due to the addition of molasses.

Citrus fruits—The juice, segments, and zest of a grapefruit, lemon, lime, and orange are refreshing to use in stir-fries, marinades, and desserts. They are great source of antioxidants.

Coconut milk—The milk from pressed coconut flesh acts as a natural sweetener in many Asian, Hawaiian, Caribbean, and South American dishes.

Fish sauce—Made of dried, fermented fish. Great to enhance stir-fry dishes.

Hoisin—A thick reddish-brown sauce, also called Peking sauce, used in not only Chinese cuisine, but in all types of Asian recipes.

Honey—The natural sweetener made by busy bees from flowering blossom nectar. A half a teaspoon will serve in your sweet recipes as the correct flavor-enhancer.

Hot sauce—A sauce made from hot peppers to spice up dishes. A few drops will do the job.

Ketjap—A darker, thicker and sweeter soy sauce indigenous to Indonesia.

Kirsch—An example of a brandy made from cherries. Makes your stir-fry desserts savory.*

Kikkoman—Popular brand of stir-fry sauces, stir-fry seasonings, soy sauces, and great flavor-enhancers.

Madeira—A pale golden fortified wine, named after the Portuguese island Madeira, is the lightest version; the darker version is the sweetest. Delicious in stir-fries, marinades, and desserts.*

Mirin—A fundamental, Japanese cooking rice wine. Adds sweetness and flavor.*

Miso—Thick paste of fermented soybeans, varying in flavor: pale yellow–mild, red–salty, and brown–stronger flavored.

Mustard—Mustard seeds, crushed fresh, mustard powder, or the blended condiment made from mustard seeds, can be used as a meat rub to add a bit of a pungent flavor.

Oil—See page 4 for more information about the different types of oil and their stir-fry ability.

Oyster sauce—Brown sauce made from oysters, seasoning, and soy sauce. Great for additional flavor.

Palm sugar—This sugar is used in Asian recipes. Often made of a combination of palm sugar and cane sugar juices.

Pam—The original or olive oil no-stick cooking spray is ideal for stir-frying any type of food.

Port—A sweet, fortified wine, indigenous to Portugal. Delicious to use with pork, poultry, or meat stir-fries. Adding a little orange juice and port to a stir-fry makes a delicious dish.*

Quick rice options—Uncle Ben's and Zatarain's are great options for a quick rice preparation. Ready in 60-90 seconds.

Rum—Rum, especially flavored rum, is great to add a little exotic aroma to your stir-fries.*

Sake—A yellowish, semi-sweet Japanese wine, traditionally served warm in cute porcelain cups. Great flavor addition to stir-fries and marinades.*

Sambal—Indonesian hot sauce with freshly crushed red peppers as the main ingredient. Sambal oelek is the base: red pepper and salt. Adding ingredients changes the name of the sambal: sambal trassie has trassie (dried shrimp paste) added; sambal katjang has freshly ground peanuts added, etc.

Seaweed—A name applied to almost any plant-like marine organism large enough to be seen with the unaided eye. Seaweed can be found growing in underwater beds, floating on the sea surface, attached to rocks and piers, and washed up on shore. Many seaweeds are rich in vitamins and minerals and are eaten in various parts of the world in soups, salads, and used as garnish.

Soy sauce—A dark sauce made from fermented soy beans. The low sodium version is ideal to season stir-fries, soups, and marinades.

Stock—Preferably freshly made for soups and stews, but in stir-fries a small amount of a good quality veggie, beef, fish, or chicken stock is okay to use. Check label to make sure the stock is low sodium or make your own .

Sugar—Hawaiian sugar, also called "Sugar in the raw," is a delicious light brown sugar.

Tapioca—A root starch derived from the cassava, or yucca plant, used to thicken and sweeten sauces.

Trassie—A paste made from ground, fermented small shrimp. The paste is pressed into block shapes. The intense aroma pears when cooked, leaving a beautiful flavor.

Vinegar—Available in a wide variety of flavors. Great to make your own dressings and marinades.

Water chestnut—A tuber vegetable that looks like a chestnut. Used in many cuisines, and great in stir-fries.

Watermelon juice—Use a juicer to make a refreshing juice to add to salad dressings and stir-fries.

Wine—Red and white wine are beautiful flavor-enhancers for marinades and stir-fries.*

* Using alcoholic liquids in food adds great flavor, and the alcohol evaporates, when stirred for at least 1 minute.

Kitchen Tools & Techniques

"Good tools are half the work!"

There are a lot of great tools that will make the

job of preparing food much easier.

A Few Great Kitchen Tools

Better Basting Brush

Good tools really make your PREP time shorter and the job easier:

Better Basting Brushes—Strong, durable, and withstands heat up to 574°F. Ideal for basting your food and applying a little oil to a stir-fry pan or wok.

Breville Juicer—The juicer is an ideal tool for extracting juice from fruit, roots, herbs, and vegetables. You can make a fruit or veggie shake for breakfast or as a snack or use a juice extract from ginger roots as a base for a dressing or sauce. The juicer is great formaking your own herbal extracts. The juice from a bunch of cilantro or basil is a great flavor-enhancher to a stir-fry.

Breville

Juicer

Chef's knife—The largest, most powerful hand tool in the kitchen. This multi-task knife has a wide blade and is used for any type of chore, no matter the size of the food item. Available in different sizes to fit your hand.

Cleaver—This Chinese tool is ideal for cutting, precision chopping, mincing, and slicing. The flat side can be used for pounding meat to flatten it to a desired thinness.

Cleaver

Food Saver—This great tool helps preserve the freshness and flavor of dry goods, produce, and other favorite foods with just the push of a button. It is much cheaper to buy meat and seasonal veggies in bulk. Cut them into the desired size (strips or bite-size) and portion it into Food Saver bags. Freeze them or store them in the fridge untill you are ready to use them.

Food Saver

Genius Onion & Veggie Cutter—Slice through onions in a matter of seconds—without tears. Just place a peeled and halved onion onto the Genius Cutter's square pegs and press the cutting sieve down. Diced pieces quickly fall into a transparent storage container. This handy kitchen helper is excellent for other vegetables as well as fruits and cheeses.

Genius Onion & Veggie Cutter

Genius Mushroom Cutter—For those hard-to-cut foods, rely on this handy unit. It's just the thing for cutting mushrooms and slicing and dicing other foods like radishes, kiwi, and eggs. Perfect for making salads and appetizers or for preparing stir-fried vegetables because it cuts in uniform sizes. Simply place the food on the blades, use gentle pressure, and press the top and bottom of the cutter together.

Magic Knife—This all-purpose adjustable cutting knife with fork makes dicing, peeling, and slicing fast and easy. The cutting guide can be easily adjusted to any desired thickness.

Magic Knife

Mandolin—A versatile tool for grating different sizes and slices of cabbage, carrots, ginger, soft cheeses, etc. The different cutting inserts make it possible to julienne (sticks), slice, or make small wafers.

Measuring Spoons—The basic tools: 1 cup, ½ cup, ⅓ cup, ¼ cup, 1 T, 1 t, ½ t and ⅓ t , and some sets have the cute, more specialized sizes: dash, pinch, smidge.

Meatball Magic—Make your own meatballs, evenly shaped, in seconds! This tool turns your favorite ground meats into nine balls of uniform size that will all cook evenly. Place the meatballs in one of the stackable containers. The containers can be frozen, so you can buy ground meat in bulk and store them in the refrigerator or freezer. They'll be ready to go when you need them.

Mortar & pestle—Available in different sizes and shapes, but all used to grind nuts or seeds and pulverize herbs and spices to the desired consistency.

Paring knife—A basic knife used for peeling, scoring, cutting, and small slicing jobs.

Peeler—Peelers are ideal for removing the skins of carrots, mangoes, parsnip, and potatoes. Some peelers are equipped with a julienne attachment to easily make julienned strips.

Pineapple Corer/Slicer—An ingenious plastic slicer that peels, cores, and slices your fresh pineapple in less than 30 seconds.

Spatula—Heat-resistant rubber is ideal for stirring, mixing, and folding in ingredients. Your spatulas should be heat resistant up to at least 450°F.

Tongs—Tools should make your life easy, and when using good quality non-stick pans, using metal tongs is not a problem.

Whisk—Hand tool to quickly mix some ingredients.

Wok—The original wok is made of season iron and holds onto the flavor of the seasonings. Besides the stove-top wok, which comes in stainless steel or with a non-stick coating, there is also an electric wok. The advantage of this is that you can set it on the desired temperature. Most electric woks have a non-stick, scratch-resistant coating that doesn't retain the seasonings, which is an advantage when "wokking" a variety of cuisines with different spices.

The pan, featured on this page, is the Cook's Essential Stainless Steel 14" Skillet. This type of skillet is ideal for stir-fry dishes. It is metal utensil-safe due to the DuPont's nonstick ScratchGuard. The skillet has a tempered-glass, stainless-steel high-domed lid, phenolic cool-touch handles, and the removable temperature probe can be set from simmer to 420°F.

Wok accessories:

Brass skimmer—A skimmer with a wooden handle to remove ingredients from hot cooking liquid.

Lid—When using a lid, your wok can be used for steaming and braising.

Ring—The ring is used to stabilize round bottom woks on the stove.

Steam plate—A flat aluminum plate, used for steaming vegetables and dumplings.

Tempura rack—The rack can be used to place fried tempura to keep it warm, or soft veggies to prevent them from getting too well done, while other food items still need a few minutes.

Zester—For zesting citrus rind, hard cheese, whole spices, and fresh ginger.

Magic Meatball

Mortar & pestle

Pineapple Corer

Spatula

Cook's Essential Electric Skillet

Zester

Knife Cuts

To ensure even cooking, try to cut the ingredients in equal shapes and size. It is no problem to have small diced and batonnet sticks, because they have the same thickness. Here are a few examples of most commonly used culinary knife cuts:

Diced squares:		Cut sticks are:	
Large dice	¾" x ¾" x ¾"	Batonnet	¼" x ¼" x 2"
Medium dice	⅓" x ⅓" x ⅓"	Allumette	⅛" x ⅛" x 1½"
Small dice	¼" x ¼" x ¼"	Julienne	¹⁄₁₆" x ¹⁄₁₆" x 1"
Brunoise	⅛" x ⅛" x ⅛"		

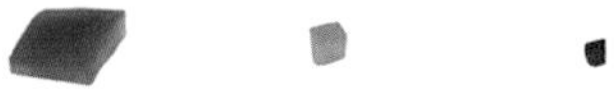

Specialty cuts:

Paysanne ½" x ½" x ⅛"

Tournee 2" x 7" sides (football)

Rondelle ⅛" to ½"

On the Bias—any size cut on the diagonal.

Chop—cut into small pieces with Chef's knife or cleaver.

Minced—food chopped into even smaller pieces.

Rings—Onions and peppers can be cut into rings.

A Few Culinary Terms

Blanch—Submerge hard vegetables into boiling water for a few minutes, then dip into cold water to stop the cooking process or add to the stir-fry pan.

Build flavor—Two ways to infuse flavors: slowly on a low temperature, like in soups and stews, or fast on a high temperature, like with stir-frying.

Bouquet garni—A leek leaf is the wrap around fresh thyme, parsley stems, and a celery stalk.

Chiffonade—This term is used for cutting leafy veggies and herbs. Remove the core or hard stems. Roll up one or more leaves, then slice lengthwise into thin strips. This method is great for stir-fry veggies, like different types of cabbage and large leaf herbs.

Holy Trinity—Cajun mire poix: celery, green pepper, onion.

Mire-Poix—Celery, leek, white onion, diced the same size.

On the bias—Cut vegetables on a diagonal to create more cooking surface.

Sachet d'épice—Bay leaf, juniper berries, dried parsley, rosemary, thyme, whole cloves, placed in a piece of cheese cloth, tied with kitchen twine.

Sauté—The fast cooking process of using a little fat/oil over high heat to allow meat to form a thin crust. Do do not move meat too quickly.

A Few Examples

Bouquet Garni

Sache d'épice

Skim the scum (depouille)—Using a large slotted spoon, removing the scum (foam) from a stock.

Shock—Submerge blanched vegetables in cold water to stop the cooking process.

Stir-fry—A traditionally Chinese cooking technique using high heat, equally cut items, with little fat and a very short cooking time, while keeping the food items moving to prevent burning and sticking to the pan. This technique assures the least loss of vitamins, minerals, and flavor.

Sweat—A cooking process to soften food items, mostly veggies, in a little fat.

Reduction—Allowing a soup, sauce, or stock to simmer on low heat to intensify the flavor by reducing the volume.

Remouillage—Means "re-wetting." After a stock is drained, add water or stock to cover the starting ingredients again, bring to a simmer. This secondary stock is being used as a cooking liquid.

Preparing Your Own Stock

Making your own stock is another way to know what is in your food, and it takes less time than you think. It is also an easy way to use stems and scraps from vegetables and herbs.

Standard ingredients for stock:

1 medium size carrot, cut rondelle; 2 celery stalks, sliced; 1 leek, sliced; 1 cup mushroom, sliced; 1 large onion, medium diced, 1 bouquet garni; 1 Sachet d'espice; 1 or 2 garlic cloves, sliced (optional).

A Few Examples

Standard PREP procedure:

Place all ingredients in the pan, add water. Bring to a rolling boil, then reduce to a simmer. Each stock has its own simmer time. Strain the stock, place in pan or container, and place in an ice bath to cool speedily, stirring occasionally. Stock can be stored in the refrigerator for a few days or frozen for ± 3–4 months.

Fish stock ingredients

Asian stock—Add garlic, ginger, and scallions. Simmer time depends on what base stock preparation you add this to.

Fish stock

Beef stock—Roast beef bones first, add mire poix. When roasted, place in stock pan. Add an acid (tomato, wine, citrus, brandy) to the pan to extract all flavor into the stock. Ratio ½ lb. to 1 gallon of water. Simmer time: ± 24 Hours.

Chicken stock—wash chicken bones and carcass; add water, vegetables, and seasonings. Add 1 diced tomato (optional). Simmer time: ± 6 hours.

Fish stock—Fish bones, fish head, mire poix, seasonings, water. To prevent the stock from getting a bitter flavor, do not boil and let simmer for a maximum of 50 minutes.

Result: a beautifully flavored shellfish stock

Shellfish stock—The shells and heads of shrimps, lobster, and crayfish are ideal for a flavorful shellfish stock. To prevent the stock from getting a bitter flavor, do not boil and let simmer for a maximum of 1½ hours.

Veggie stock—Use herbal stems, vegetable scraps, and seasonings. To prevent the stock from losing its nutritional value and from turning bitter, let simmer for a maximum of 50 minutes.

Index & References

Recipe Index

Vegetables (specialty)	25	
• Broccoli raab	25	• Kohlrabi	25
• Choy sum	25		

• Soft Vegetables: artichoke hearts, Azuki beans, bean sprouts, beets, Belgium endive, black beans, bok choy (leafy part), chickpeas, corn, cucumber, eggplant (Brazilian, Italian, Japanese, purple, Thai, white), fiddlehead fern, kidney beans, legumes, lentils, lima beans, mushrooms, napa cabbage, pinto beans, pole beans, savoy cabbage, soybeans, spinach, squash, and tomato.

• Hard vegetables: asparagus, bell pepper, bok choy (white part), broccoli, broccoli raab, brussels sprouts, cabbage (Chinese, red, etc.), carrots, celery, celeriac, choy sum, collard greens, cranberry beans, daikon, fava beans, fennel bulb, green beans, haricot verts, jicama, kale, kohlrabi, long beans, onion, peas, potato, radishes, seeds, snow peas, sugar snap peas, and yellow wax beans.

Research

The research for this book consists of many international studies and organizations on this page that have been helpful, interesting, resourceful and gave important information to share with you to educate you and to help you live healthier.

- Franz, Marion J. "Protein Controversies in Diabetes." *Diabetes Spectrum*, Volume 13, Number 3, 2,000, pages 132-141. (http://journal.diabetes.org/diabetesspectrum/00v13n3/pg132.htm)
- Foster-Powell, K., and Miller, J. B. (1995) International tables of glycemic index. *American Journal of Clinical Nutrition* 62, S871-S890
- Brand Miller, Janette, et al. "Rice: a High or Low Glycemic Index Food?" *The American Journal of Clinical Nutrition*, Vol. 56, 1992, pp. 1034-1036.
- Glycemic Research Institute, www.glycemic.com
- National Center for Chronic Disease Prevention and Health Promotion, www.cdc.gov/diabetes/
- Ludwig, D. S., Majzoub, J. A., Al-Zahrani, A., Dallal, G. E., Blanco, I., and Roberts, S. B. (1999) High glycemic index foods, overeating, and obesity. *Pediatrics 103*, art. no.-e26 (http://www.pediatrics.org/cgi/content/full/103/3/e26)
- Functional Foods for Health, www.ag.uiuc.edu/ffh/research_updates.html
- The World of Food Science, www.worldfoodscience.org/cms/
- EU Childhood Obesity Programme, www.childhood-obesity.org
- U.S. Food and Drug Administration, www.cfsan.fda.gov/list.html

Reference & Interesting Links

- The Alzheimer Association. National Office, 225 N. Michigan Ave., Fl. 17, Chicago, IL 60601 24/7 Nationwide Contact Center: 1.800.272.3900 www.alz.org/
- National Eating Disorder Association, 603 Stewart St., Suite 803, Seattle, WA 98101 (206) 382-3587 www.nationaleatingdisorders.org.
- American Heart Association, National Center, 7272 Greenville Avenue, Dallas, TX 75231 www.americanheart.org

Culinary References

- Amoy Food Limited, www.amoy.com
- PomWonderful, www.pomwonderful.com
- *Culinary Artistry*, Dornenburg, A. and Page, K.
- *The Modern Art of Chinese Cooking Techniques & Recipes*, Tropp, B.

Why You Have to Watch Your Glycemic Index

As we already indicated in the intro pages, six nutrients are necessary for the proper functioning of your body. That is why you should not cut out carbohydrates, but adjust them to your needs. Remember the 80-20 rule: combining 80 percent low-glycemic food items with 20 percent high-glycemic food items to balance your blood sugar level.

Eating mainly low-glycemic food results in:

- A smaller rise in blood glucose levels after meals and snacks.
- A decrease in the sensitivity of the body to insulin, which will improve the control of diabetes.
- A less "bumpy road" makes it easier to stay on the right path to healthy weight loss. When the body is in balance, it doesn't suffer from hunger and cravings, and keeping control of your food intake is easier, which results in weight loss and weight management.

High-Glycemic Food items	Low-Glycemic Food Items	
Apricots	Agave nectar	Lentils
Bananas (especially ripened)	Apple	Limes
Bagels	Artichoke hearts	Kidney beans
Carrot, cooked	Barley	Oranges
Cornflakes	Bell peppers	Pancakes made with integral
Donuts	Berries	wheat flour
French fries	Black beans	Peaches
Glucose	Black rice	Peanuts
Honey	Broccoli	Pears
Maltose	Bulgar	Plums
Mango	Cabbage	Pomegrates
Pancakes made with refined flour	Celery	Snap beans
Parsnip, cooked	Cherries	Snow peas
Potatoes	Collard greens	Summer squash
Raisins	Couscous	Rice bran
Refined breakfast cereal	Cranberries	Soybeans
Soft drinks	Cucumbers	Strawberries
Sucrose	Currants	Tomatoes
Sugar	Eggplant	Watercress
White bread	Fructose	Whole fruits
White rice, pasta, and noodles	Grapefruit	Whole grain breakfast cereal
	Most legumes	Whole vegetables, blanched
	Mushrooms	Whole wheat, Oats, Bran
	Lemons	Whole grain pastas and noodles
		Yogurt

Diet Myth **As you can see, the choices for low-glycemic foods are healthy choices, but foods in the high-glycemic list also contain lots of healthy nutrients. A healthy diet is a variety of delicious food in moderation!**